Reflections

ADVANCE PRAISE FOR *REFLECTIONS*

'An important book that will focus minds on the consequences of misunderstanding water and how we can change our perceptions and actions.'
—**Tristan Gooley**, author of *How to Read Water*

'Prof Zeitoun provides us with an elegant call for civility in the ways we individually and collectively deal with one of our most precious resources. Essential to the future of humankind—indeed instrumental in determining our potential horizons, he escorts us back and forth between the ways we feel about water and the things we do with it—revealing unpleasant truths about our collective use and abuse of and through water. Whether it is taken for granted or the underlying cause of wars, treated as commonplace or hoarded selfishly, water is critical to our futures in ways eloquently explained and illustrated in this rewarding read.'
—**Jamie Bartram**, Professor Emeritus, University of North Carolina at Chapel Hill

Mark Zeitoun's most recent book offers a highly informative and convincingly argued set of reflections on water. It leads the reader beyond the simplistic truisms about water into the world of social complexity, the insatiable thirst for power, and the brutality of armed conflicts. He argues that human ingenuity is using water 'in impressively clever and incredibly myopic ways.' Can this change? Yes, it can, and there are elements of a more farsighted approach visible in the evolution of international law. However, real progress will require a better understanding of water, and the present book will help.
—**Danilo Türk**, Former President of the Republic of Slovenia and Chairman of the Global High Level Panel on Water and Peace

'Zeitoun's book reflecting on water use and abuse is a highly readable and accessible account of the complexities surrounding a topic which is fundamental to all our lives. It spans politics, history, sociology, philosophy, and law, as well as the practicalities of managing water and how this has evolved over time. It serves as an excellent primer for both specialists and non-specialists on an increasingly pertinent topic that interplays with climate change, armed conflict, and health—something that is increasingly relevant as waterborne diseases, their drivers, and their impacts affect the most vulnerable in our societies.'
—**Aula Abarra**, Honorary Clinical Senior Lecturer, Imperial College London

Reflections

Understanding Our Use and Abuse of Water

Mark Zeitoun

Oxford University Press is a department of the University of Oxford. It furthers
the University's objective of excellence in research, scholarship, and education
by publishing worldwide. Oxford is a registered trade mark of Oxford University
Press in the UK and certain other countries.

Published in the United States of America by Oxford University Press
198 Madison Avenue, New York, NY 10016, United States of America.

© Oxford University Press 2023

All rights reserved. No part of this publication may be reproduced, stored in
a retrieval system, or transmitted, in any form or by any means, without the
prior permission in writing of Oxford University Press, or as expressly permitted
by law, by license, or under terms agreed with the appropriate reproduction
rights organization. Inquiries concerning reproduction outside the scope of the
above should be sent to the Rights Department, Oxford University Press, at the
address above.

You must not circulate this work in any other form
and you must impose this same condition on any acquirer.

Library of Congress Control Number: 2022950549
ISBN 978–0–19–757512–3

DOI: 10.1093/oso/9780197575123.001.0001

Printed by Integrated Books International, United States of America

To Tony Allan and all others who reflect when they throw stones into water

Acknowledgements

The bulk of this book was written from within the ever-shrinking walls of a flat at the height of a global pandemic. Water bodies that I used to examine and play in seemed at that time to be as distant as any wilful optimism I had of the future. I have since managed to look again at puddles from interesting angles again, stare straight up at the rain, peer into wet caves, and splash back into rivers—and I have found many things to admire about the way we relate to and use water. But these will have to wait for the next book. The thoughts on these pages thus remain lockdown-induced reflections of several decades of critical observation and analytical cynicism, fuelled by belief that calling out follies and injustices improves things.

I am indebted to editors Madeline Long and Mary-Lou Zeitoun, who warmed and smithed my frozen thoughts to help them flow. I am also forever grateful to and inspired by my very many family members, friends, teachers, students, and colleagues who consistently demonstrate the courage and moral commitment to be curious and bold, and to swim against the mainstream. Samia and Adam not least of all.

Contents

Abbreviations	xi
Introduction: Beneath the Surface	**1**
1. Misunderstood Water	**7**
Water cycles	9
Water problems are local	15
Scarcity is constructed	17
Rain is commodified	18
2. Insatiable Thirst	**20**
The mission	21
Hydraulic societies	21
The supply	23
The infrastructure	25
Lubricating colonisation	30
The thirst	33
Water for the wealthy	34
From crops per drop to dollars per drop	37
Desert bloom syndrome	40
Not solutions	42
Shade balls	43
Desalting the sea to bloom the desert	44
Sugar water	46
Bottled water	47
3. Killer Water	**51**
Everlasting conflict	52
A tool of war	55
Hunting thirsty gazelles	55
Clearing the killing fields	58
Ethnic cleansing	59
A target of war	62
Cumulative impact	62
Spreading disease	65
Toxic biospheres of war	68
The Rules of War	70

4. Hostile Waters — 74
    Why we don't wage war over water — 75
    Why we don't wage peace over water — 77
        Confusing correlation with causation — 77
        Lazy thinking about 'cooperation' — 79
    Why we do fight over water — 81
    Hoarding on the Tigris and Euphrates — 82
    Hoarding on the Nile — 85
    Hoarding on the Jordan — 90
    The rules for sharing water — 93

Conclusion: Water Whilst It Is in Our Hands — 96

Bibliography — 103
Index — 115

Abbreviations

AHD	Aswan High Dam DIU—Sudanese Dams Implementation Unit
GERD	Grand Ethiopian Renaissance Dam
ICWE	International Conference on Water and the Environment
IHL	International Humanitarian Law
IR	International Relations
IWL	International Water Law
JWC	Joint Water Committee (Palestinian–Israeli)
LAPDW	Los Angeles Department of Water and Power
MOU	Memorandum of Understanding
NBI	Nile Basin Initiative
PLO	Palestine Liberation Organisation
PWA	Palestinian Water Authority
RO	Reverse osmosis
TVA	Tennessee Valley Authority
UNECE	United Nations Economic Commission for Europe
UNSC	United Nations Security Council
USAID	United States Agency for International Development
WCD	World Commission on Dams

Introduction

Beneath the Surface

> You can never enter the same river twice, for it is not the same river, and you are not the same person.
> —Heraclitus, Fragments of Heraclitus, B49a

Source: Author.

I want you to think deeply about water. You could start by considering the way that water reflects whatever our eyes make of what is on its surface. The way a lake or sea casts back an image of a bright and high moon or a mildly setting sun. When the surface is perfectly calm, water gives a near-mirror image. If the surface is even the slightest little bit disturbed, the shine travels along the surface all the way from the horizon to your feet or the shore. Standing in the glow of this 'glitter path' at sunset or very late at night quiets the mind like nothing short of a crackling campfire.[1]

Water surfaces are rarely so calm, however. More often than not, the veneer is disturbed by the wind, birds dipping in, boats motoring across, the arcing 'plop' of stones thrown by children, or minnows and bigger things lurking beneath. The reflection is a significant distortion of what we observe directly. When they are reflected on the surface, the mountains or trees or houses which line the shore can look like they are going through an earthquake in a time warp. Even in urban rivers, the colours and rays of light from lampposts, apartment blocks, and car headlights merge on the surface into some sort of live oil painting.

Our minds apply their own filters, naturally, and we see in the reflection what we want to see. Where I romanticise a cityscape, you might be put off entirely. Many people tend to view the reflection literally, automatically filling in the noise created by the ripples with what their cognition tells them must be there, or what *should* be there if the image were true. Others will readily imagine much of what they see as the logical side of their brain gives way to memories and smells of childhood or departed loved ones. Narcissus saw himself—but a better version of himself. Some see kelpies or sea dragons or gods in the water, then extract explanations of 'real' world phenomena.

No matter the image thrown back at us, it always at least partly reflects our personalities. Sometimes we will let crystal-clear water inspire us and ignore the fact that the clarity is evidence of a deprived ecosystem. Other times, we will look away from the glittering path to the pipe spewing sewage into the river or to the clouds or fields that transport acid and fertilisers into it and wonder what to do about it. Our inaction, handwringing, or actions are reflections of society writ large.

Of course, water reflects the best and worst of humanity. At this moment, I do not particularly like what I see, so I draw most of your attention to the latter. I see an abundance of clean water enjoyed by some and denied to many. I see how we disrupt the way that nature cleanses itself and all who depend on it. I see rivers pitting communities against each other as the fiercest of rivals. I see the source of most myths about human creation used to destroy. Like a critical mirror, water reveals that the harm we can inflict on nature and ourselves has no limits.

Water is, some may say in essence, nourishing, cleansing, and unifying. I do not think there is anything inherent in water that transcends interpretations of our relationship with it, not for a second. Still, we project these abstract qualities on water such that they can never be separated from the material ones, though we do our best to try. Water fully and completely sustains our bodies: it always has done. Rivers have flowed before we are born and will long after we go. Aquifers have sustained life for billions of years and will continue long after whatever epoch is to follow the

---

[1] Gooley, *How to Read Water: Clues and Patterns from Puddles to the Sea.*

Anthropocene. More than just life! Water nourishes our minds when it stimulates thought and our souls when it inspires art. The water cycle has forever nourished, and will for evermore. But when I see how frequently we deny water to those who cannot afford it, I must conclude that water says less about our will to nourish, and more about our capacity for greed and depravation. Having witnessed the effects of pulverised pumping stations on war-torn populations, it is clear to me that we use water to create thirst as much as we do to satiate it.

The evidence obliges that we critically examine the extent to which water can cleanse and unify, too. Water can wash away all the nasties in the world, just about. Pure H_2O is perfectly sterile. Imagine the COVID-19 pandemic without water to wash your hands. Think about the fact that your great-grandfather had to poo in a toilet without plumbing. People of his time generally died decades earlier than their offspring because of the disease that lurked in their drinking water. Indeed, the great strides we have taken to improve public health is a story of water. Ever since the pump at Broad Street was identified as the source of cholera in London in the 1800s, we have protected our water sources from contamination and built sewers to get our waste as far away from us as possible. Water science and infrastructure have, without a doubt, improved the quality of billions of lives. Yet, even today, industrial particulates emitted into the clouds join rain drops falling onto farmers' fields, mix with pesticides as they stream into rivers, then link up with the endocrine-disrupters and remnants of feel-good drugs we have ejected from our bodies. Water treatment plants do not even measure for these things, much less treat them. Groundwater is poisoned by the leftovers of mines dug in our quest for heavy metals for our phones. Many aquifers that have stored water safely since the Stone Age will become contaminated beyond repair within a decade. Too many rivers on every continent are not just too filthy to drink, they are even too toxic to wade in.

At least water remains a great leveller and unifier, right? It does not decide who or what it nourishes or cleanses. Watering holes in deserts attract all manner of beasts, predators and prey, binding them in a pact that is as ancient as it is temporary. People who live on the same lake but in different countries share their cultures and co-clean their commons. People of all classes arrive at the same fishing spot and can talk about angling as easily as they do about TV series or football. Yet water also seems to catalyse fierce allegiances to tribe or flag. Canadians quietly reach for their ice hockey sticks when their downstream American neighbours suggest some transboundary lakes be shared, just as many of the latter firmly deny water to downstream farmers in Mexico.

Such a reaction by people who generally view themselves as nature-loving may be a leftover of the poisoned clouds that discharge acid rain. They react without a thought to the extreme violence that created the political borders that the rivers themselves mark. In fact, water creates a sense of geographic nationalism in the most liberal of people. The juggernaut of emotions over water overwhelms rationale in the Congo River Basin, in the Jordan River Basin, and just about every place that is soaking wet or dry as a bone. Whatever our intents and faults, it is *we* who decide who and what water nourishes and cleanses, and we use it to divide more than to unify.

I seek through this book to make sense of the lengths we go to as we bend water's abstract and life-affirming qualities to destructive ends and the extent to which we deny this fact to ourselves. The impetus started soon after I and two dozen other bright and conforming youngsters had been infused with unwarranted confidence by a degree in civil engineering from an institution that has produced some of the world's most illustrious dam-builders. Our teachers had been taught that nature could be conquered for the sake of man with a little bit of physics and a lot of reinforced concrete. They taught us that the goal was to restore nature for all humanity, with a little biology and a lot of reinforced concrete. The oath we took when we graduated[2] committed us to serve the public. For the engineers who specialised in hydraulics, this meant making water available for others by cleaning and pumping it.

It was more than just circumstance, then, when an international nongovernmental organisation (NGO) sent me to implement water-saving campaigns in the Palestinian West Bank. I knew that it did not rain a lot there, that more efficient use of water would ease the effects of the scarcity, and that using less water would support the negotiations that were going to bring peace between Palestinians and Israelis. I knew the problem, I knew the solution, and I had the toolkit to play my part.

One of the so-called beneficiaries of our project was an elderly lady who lived in a small breeze-block hut with a tin roof amongst the hills south of Hebron. The land was parched because no rain falls throughout the entire (northern hemispheric) summer months. But it rains quite a lot in the winter, I found out—as much as it does in London in an entire year. All four of her sons worked in the nearby city, and she provided for the remaining family by raising goats, chickens, and herbs. Like so many who live on the shores of the Mediterranean, she made *labneh*, or pressed yoghurt, draining the whey out by hanging it in a permeable cheesecloth. The yoghurt came from the milk of the goats who grazed the scarce clover on the parched brown soil all summer. She caught the whey-charged drainage water in a bucket, gave some to her chickens and the rest to her herbs. She was caring for every drop exceptionally efficiently. I had nothing to teach her. But a lot to learn.

Still hoping to be useful, I tossed my book of clever water-saving tips aside and suggested she catch and store the winter rains somehow, to tide her over the dry months. She explained to me that her sons had once spent a month working the ground around her home into terraces to channel the rain overland into an underground cistern. But then the soldiers ('the men with the guns' she called them) came and destroyed their work in minutes. Being Palestinian, she has few rights in the land where her family has long lived. Capturing the rain is not one of them. Meanwhile, settlers who had

---

[2] All who graduate from engineering schools in Canada follow Rudyard Kipling's 'Ritual of the Calling of an Engineer' upon their graduation. The ritual obliges them to use their skills to 'serve humanity by making best use of the Earth's precious wealth.' It does not encourage them to explore the extent to which Kipling limited 'humanity' to a particular type of people nor to question the imperial assumptions behind the mission he laid out (as George Orwell does in his essay 'Rudyard Kipling').

taken over the land less than two kilometres away were maintaining industrial-grade agriculture and livestock farms through a very secure supply of water piped by the Israeli government.

I hated but had to admit that the extent of my ignorance was matched only by the degree of my arrogance. I also realised just how substandard my excellent education was in preparing me for geopolitical conflicts. My degree obliged me to use water to help others, but I was not equipped even to consider how some people use water efficiently without the help of anybody else. Nothing in the engineering curriculum explained *why* some people are forced to eke out their life in this way while their neighbours enjoy all the comfort that most of us have come to expect. And nobody taught me that some people use water not to help others but to force them from the land.

Once I had pulled the tail out from between my legs, I stopped taking water's abstract and beautiful qualities for granted. I have since learned to question why we use water to contaminate, to starve, and to divide, instead of to cleanse, to nourish, and to unite. I find this deeper, darker side of water almost everywhere I look with an almost monotonous predictability. Shrunken lakes, dead rivers, poisoned aquifers, dry taps, shot-up water towers, perforated pipelines—and people benefitting and suffering from the actions in equal measure.

The central point to this book is the dissonance between how we see and feel about water and what we do with it. One way to explore the dichotomy is to confront the paradox that it creates. Many of us claim that water is the world's most precious resource, that it has the most exquisite of essential qualities, and that we hold it dear. Yet we give it little meaningful value, betray its essence at every turn, and treat it like a shoddy throwaway. We think we use water in a civilised manner, towards compassionate ends. But, in truth, 'barbaric' is a better description of the way many of us behave.

The explanation of the water paradox frames the rest of this book (localised mostly in Western Asia, where most of my observations were made). First, we do not really understand water, despite its ubiquity. If our brains are ever switched on to the topic, they turn off soon afterwards. As we discuss in Chapters 1 and 2, this makes us feel good about some things we do with water (like turn off the tap when brushing our teeth) but remain ignorant of the consequences of others (like the impact that drinking Coke has on freshwater biomes). Where water comes from and where it goes is someone else's concern, not ours. We have no clue about how much water is required to grow an eggplant or a cow, or what an important and tricky accomplishment it is to treat our sewage.

We mythologise water, instead. We assert, again and again, that 'water is life' in opinion pieces and essays or when attracting research funds. We comfort ourselves with truisms like water abundance leads to peace or that water scarcity leads to war. Both the optimistic and cynical assertions satisfy our desire to oversimplify and find causality within complex relationships. But dreamers and determinists alike should take heed: as discussed in Chapter 2, there are few universal truths that water does not dissolve. Fully functioning water systems may look all shiny and useful but can veil tensions that are driven by highly asymmetric control of water and stress about water 'needs' that have been fabricated by those who have gamed the politics and economics to their favour.

The third explanation of the paradox concerns the political-economic system within which the water experts and decision-makers operate. The interests and incentives which have been created in the political economy of water are readily understood if we accept that water is treated as a commodity: a resource that can be produced, packaged, distributed, sold, traded, or denied. What used to be rain becomes water, the way that the wooden fork strapped to your biodegradable plastic take-away salad dish was once a tree.

Once rain or clouds or rivers are commodified, water becomes an artifact to be exploited in the pursuit of profit (Chapter 2), war (Chapter 3), and domestic and political agendas (Chapters 1 and 4). The profits come from generating electricity, selling bottled water, privatising drinking water services, and making deserts bloom. Water serves political aims at home when states lay pipes to satisfy or kick out the resident population. It serves political aims abroad when an international watercourse is shared or hoarded. In the heat and chaos of armed conflict, water serves our military and political goals. We bomb water sources and infrastructure, we use water tactically or strategically to terrorise and kill.

The more that water serves financial, political, or violent goals, the less incentive or opportunity there is to 'know' water in any other way. So, we turn 'round the cycle. In fact, just about everything we do with water is politically sensible and economically rational. Doing anything else requires rocking the boat or putting your head above the parapet. But too many of us have not yet mustered the courage even where it is safe to do so; the rest live in areas where it would be far too dangerous.

Nothing in the three-point logic of the explanation of the paradox suggests that we should use *less* water, but everything in it compels us to reflect on *how* we use water. That is, what do we do with water for those moments that it is in our hands. We will continue to desecrate water's essential qualities as long as we do not reflect upon our assumptions about it. We will continue to pollute where we could be cleansing. We will divide and deny instead of unifying and providing. Understanding water will not provide magic answers, but it can illuminate the path to finding them. For if we are ready to delve deeply enough, we can develop an informed ethos of water—a culture of care based on a solid understanding of water and just how clearly our use of it reflects ourselves.

1
Misunderstood Water

> The sound of water made me terribly thirsty.... When I reached the river and saw it rushing past from right to left, I felt much better. At the very least, a large quantity of water was on the move. It had originated somewhere and was flowing somewhere else, filling the contours of the land. In a place here nothing stirred, and no wind blew, the sound of rushing water reverberated around me.
> —Haruki Murakami, *Killing Commendatore*

Water molecules trying to stick together when a canoe paddle is pulled out through them. Note also the glitter path and ripple patterns.
Source: Author.

8 Reflections

There may be more reasons to love water than there are grains of sand on all the world's beaches. My personal favourite is water's fascinating and delightful way of trying to stick together whenever it is disturbed. Wind produces the ripples that disturb the water's glassy surface. The light breeze, shaped by the warm pine forest it has blown through, might be the leftover edge of a tornado that touched down earlier, which may have been caused in part—you will have heard—by a butterfly flapping its wings on a continent in the other hemisphere. The ripples created then extend out in circles of ever-increasing size and decreasing energy, exposing the pond-skimmers to the fish below and disturbing the glitter path.

From a microscopic perspective, the ripple is created by the habit that H_2O molecules have of trying to remain together—small but mighty bonds pulling the molecules together. The molecules at the edges are always drawn back to the main body, pulled back down whence they came, thereby forming a ripple. This is the surface tension you learned about, the property that allows water to rise ever so slightly above the rim of a glass and pond-skimmers to skim across ponds.[1]

Water does its best to act like mercury droplets, which run across just about any surface. Water manages the performance when it is on *hydrophobic* (literally, 'water-fearing') surfaces that do not absorb it, like dew on a spider's web or a spilled drink on a wooden deck which has just been coated with weather protection. Or an ocean wave coming near shore—the bottom part of the wave slows down as the top part crests to reach its peak in beauty and energy just before it all falls apart.

The stick together-ness also explains why little eddies are created when you cleave a paddle through water as you pull your canoe forward. Just look at how much you can rip water apart when you lift the paddle out of the water, as at the start of this chapter. Drop an ice cube into a drink or throw a rock into a lake and watch and think carefully about the splash. Even when the bonds between the water molecules are fractured into the hundreds of droplets splashing onto the shore, they reestablish themselves as the drops return to the lake. Like ducklings separated from their mother. Even if you fired a missile into a lake, all the water would return to its original state before too long (and long before any of the surrounding soil, trees, houses, and minds of the children reverted to any state of 'normal').

Water can also do dazzling things with light. There is undeniable beauty in the way urban rivers reflect the bright, light green willow buds in the evening as they are illuminated by streetlights. The reflection can wildly distort the branches and leaves when the wind is blowing and the surface is choppy. Or when the surface is perfectly calm, it can reflect the buds so truthfully that you might think that it is life imitating art. Like Monet's water lilies.

---

[1] The phenomena may be even better explained by considering water in its 'gel' phase wherever it meets a water-repelling surface. The behaviour of water molecules at the margins suggests there may exist what Prof. Pollack calls a *fourth* phase of water: water that behaves more like gel than it does bulk liquid water (or ice or gas) (see, e.g., Pollack, Figueroa, and Zhao 'Molecules, water, and radiant energy'). The finding opens all sorts of possibility for tapping into the energy sorted and released there.

Some people love water because of the delightful smell of a flower garden after a gentle rain. Or because of the great relief felt when the first monsoons break the stifling heat. Or the exhilaration of the liquid cold passing over your cracked lips and dry tongue, down your parched throat. As playwright José Bergamín noted, '[T]o be thirsty and to drink water is the perfection of sensuality rarely achieved. Sometimes you drink water; other times you are thirsty.'[2] You might find joy from songbirds or gazelles enjoying a freshwater spring or water hole, or perhaps from the sensation of the energy that emanates from one river feeding another at their confluence. Children enjoy watching car window water droplets lose the fight to stay together as they bead and streak as they motor on, one racing another across the window. When any drop has a chance to join with others, they give up all pretence of independence and become one stream.

Rain drops connect all the way down their journey to the earth. Gentle rains mean low cloud cover; violent rains are from much further up. But even the rain that has collected softly on a leaf eventually connects with enough moisture to succumb to gravity and drop into a pond or puddle below—allowing you to gaze at your reflection or quench your thirst. Such is the whole of water so much bigger than the sum of its parts. If none of these grabs you personally, consider at least the fact that humans cannot survive more than a few days without water, that water is central to our health, or that we are connected with everything that has ever lived via the water cycle.

Water cycles

Here's the water cycle diagram you may have been shown first when you were six or seven years old (Figure 1.1). There are hundreds of versions of this diagram populating kids' textbooks across the globe.[3] It's time for another look. Note how water passes through each of its three phases—liquid (lake), solid (snow), gas (moisture)—as rain and snow wash off a mountain into a river through the forests and to the sea.[4] Then it takes the great return trip back up to the atmosphere, only to fall as snow or rain again.

Water has been circulating around in this way for thousands of years, and this cycle connects us with anything that has ever lived, with every drink and with every breath you take. It means what you drink today once was dinosaur pee. And future beings will be drinking what was once your urine. Fortunately, some of the cycle's funky biophysical processes remove all but the H_2O molecules, so that the rain is largely safe to drink. The scientific terms used to describe the life-giving processes are 'precipitation,' 'evaporation' (or 'transpiration'), and 'condensation.' Teachers drop these five-syllable terms on unwitting children and emphasise the cycle by spinning their hands in ever faster and tighter circles. The kids who are best at memorising the terms feel proud, but few grasp the enormous significance of this cycle a few months later.

---

[2] Attributed to José Bergamín, at www.azquotes.com.
[3] See Linton, *What Is Water?*
[4] Or is it four? See Note 1.

10 Reflections

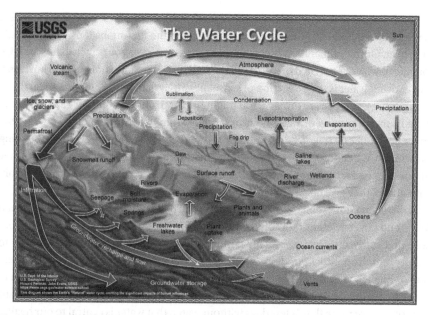

Figure 1.1 A biophysical representation of the water cycle. This diagram is taught across the world although it only accurately reflects conditions in coastal mountain zones.
Source: USGS Public Domain at https://www.usgs.gov/media/images/water-cycle-poster-natural-water-cycle

There are good reasons the water cycle is so quickly forgotten, but there are serious consequences, too. We let our understanding slip because the water cycle we have been taught is a bad simplification of reality. Notice how much the diagram looks like the Pacific coast of North America or parts of central Europe. It does not represent land-locked Afghanistan or Zimbabwe, the seasonal rains of Western Asia, or the temperamental cycles South American coasts. Neither northern, sub-Saharan, or southern Africa, nor Central or Southeast Asia. In short, the classroom water cycle represents a narrow slice of real-world geography.

The generalisation does effectively teach the principle, but imagine replacing it with a diagram that was more suited to a child's specific context. Considering how quickly irrigation water dries up in most of Jordan, for example, the summer hydrocycle diagram taught to kids in Irbid or Amman would emphasise evaporation above the other processes, and the winter hydrocycle diagram would emphasise the highly unpredictable and shifting timing of the rainfalls. Kids living in monsoon regions would draw the downwards rain arrows as ginormous bolts of lightning (as they are experienced) rather than as more delicate showers. An Amazonian hydrocycle would show the two-way exchange between trees and clouds; with such a heavy tree canopy, there is not a lot of evaporation or runoff happening in the world's most biodiverse habitat. It would certainly be easier to implement wise water-use campaign, if, a few generations from now, everyone understood how *their* hydrocycle affected their lives, rather than how one in Washington State might.

Another problem with the classic hydrocycle diagram is the selection and omission of different types of water. Rivers, lakes, and oceans get prime billing, possibly because we can see and pump this water. But when we gaze on surface water, we overlook all the groundwater that is stored and moves through aquifers (see Box 1.1), the water drawn from hand-dug wells or pumped up from deep tube wells and boreholes. Despite groundwater being responsible for the great bulk of food produced in India, Turkey, and other places, its underbilling in the classic hydrocycle diagram is wholly misleading. Like surface water, groundwater is foremost in most people's minds because this is what we drink or thirst for.

Box 1.1 In defence of aquifers

Lots of people are passionate about rivers, but few get excited about the water in the ground. Indeed, the greatest buzz most of us can muster about aquifers is when we ride a boat through the crystalline waters of limestone caverns (which are essentially underground rivers).

But there is a lot to be said for aquifers. They supply more than one-third of the water for irrigated farms worldwide and provide at least half the drinking water globally. Remember that water your great-grandfather or grandmother brought home from a well? The water lies in the cracks and crevices in the rock structure, the aquifer, drawing it, in some cases, from miles away. It's a very nice quality of drink, too, with the soil above the aquifer clearing out most of the nasties and the limestone or basalt or chalk adding the nutrients that are so central to water's nourishing qualities. What once fell as rain percolated down through the soil into the crevices and wound its way along the path for days or centuries before discharging from the aquifer at the sacred gathering point of springs.

Springs bubble out of the foothills in all the lucky parts of the world. Spring water is essentially pure groundwater that is so accessible it is practically asking us to drink it. It is usually safe because the soil that it runs through filters out most of the life-threatening pathogens and healthy to drink because the aquifer rocks it runs through dissolve into it as calcium, magnesium, and other minerals. Like the springs which provide entire communities with their supply in the Niari and other districts of the Republic of Congo, they also serve as social gathering points. In this sense, springs are the outward expression of the inner beauty of aquifers.

Bearing the forces of the signals in the political economy which govern water use, however, there is nothing in the wonderful rock structures which prevents us from extracting water from it faster than the rain recharges it or from denying it to people who need it the most.

In fact, the average adult drinks about 1,000 litres of the stuff every year, roughly three or four litres daily, but they indirectly consume about 10,000 times more water from the food they choose to eat, which either is or has eaten the plants that drew the water up from the soil. Yet soil water is only hinted at in the classic water cycle through the small arrow labelled 'plant uptake'. Soil water soaks the ground and is pulled up by the roots of plants even before it gets into the aquifers or rivers. Also referred to as 'green water', soil water is not only the main source of water for our food, but also for the vast majority of forests in the world.

With soils science very firmly relegated below to hydrological sciences, soil water gets very little space in any country's education system. The only people who really know soil water are farmers because their livelihoods depend on it. Soil water would surely garner more attention if there was a way of collecting and using it, rather than simply cultivating the food that grows in it. We would price it, store it, deny it to others, as we do with all other forms of water. Until then, though, soil water remains the domain of vegetation, soils scientists, and farmers.

On his way to becoming the world's most creative water thinker, Tony Allan coined the term 'virtual water' to draw attention to the water which is pulled up by the roots of a plant and transpired to the atmosphere through its leaves. 'Virtual water' is water in essence, if not quite in fact. The concept has wide-reaching implications for sustainable water use and geopolitics alike because states have proven more adept at securing their food import lines than managing the water that lies within their territory.

Producing things requires an enormous amount of water, as shown in Figure 1.2. Hops roots tap about one hundred and fifty litres for every pint of beer, for example. Over one thousand litres are pulled up to produce a small breast of chicken and nearly double that for a quarter-pound hamburger. If you had a ham and cheese sandwich at lunch, you ate twice as much virtual water today than you will drink of 'real' water for the next year, and you have not even had dinner yet. Bearing the cyclical nature of water in mind, our virtual water consumption does not necessarily mean that drinking more beer and eating less beef will in any way 'save' water. The moisture transpired by the leaves of the barley or feed goes back up into the clouds to fall again somewhere else, some other day. Grass, crops, and trees pull water out of the ground and release it more than one hundred metres up into the atmosphere, like giant water fountains run by the quietest of pumps, but few know where this water falls again.

The other gaping hole in the classic hydrocycle diagram is human activity. Measured in terms of weight, humans are 60 per cent water. The heart is three-quarters water, the brain, too. Water lubricates joints, helps reduce the shocks on the spinal cord, and is essential for digestion. We drink water, then excrete; we inhale it, then exhale. We are the water cycle. We affect it when we pollute the atmosphere with emissions, contaminate lakes with industrial waste or farm runoff, dam rivers and increase the evaporation rates behind the dam reservoirs, pollute the groundwater

Misunderstood Water

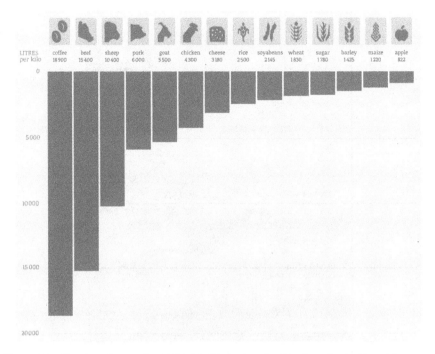

Figure 1.2 The virtual water footprint of different agricultural products. Tony Allan conceived of the idea of 'virtual water' to draw attention to just how much water is required to produce things, especially food. The bulk is accounted for by the barley or livestock fodder's transpiration of soil water back up to the atmosphere. If you have a hamburger for lunch, you will have eaten four times more virtual water today than you drank liquid water in an entire year.
Source: Angela Morelli.

with the lubricants used to fracture the rock in our pursuit of gas, or prevent rain infiltrating the soil by paving over cities. So human activity ought to be incorporated into the classroom teaching tools—better still when adapted for the students' local climate and geography.

But the extent of our influence on the water cycle can be underplayed if we do not nest it within the terms of the political economic systems we have created. We falsely assume that water obeys only the laws of nature because pumping technology allows us to reach much further down into aquifers than hand-dug wells and pump much higher than the tallest of sequoias. In fact, we can—and do—pump groundwater from hundreds of metres deep and pump it up (relatively noisily) several kilometres away to the highest of apartment blocks or hilltop houses. Every pump and reservoir in the world alters the hydrocycle in very specific and predictable ways.

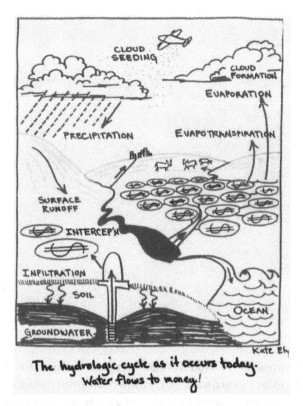

Figure 1.3 A political economic and biophysical representation of the water cycle. It emphasises how the cycle is affected by human activity, which can make 'water flow uphill towards money' (as Mark Reisner notes in his *Cadillac Desert*).
Source: Kate Ely.

We pump water to whomever can pay for it. As Mark Reisner asserts in his must-read book, *Cadillac Desert*, 'water flows towards power and money'.[5] The author tells a masterful story of how our thirst and ingenuity facilitated the greed and opportunism to create one of the world's great cities: Los Angeles.[6] If water flowed undisturbed through its cycle, LA would still be a village. But with water diverted to it from the Colorado River via massive canals in the San Joaquin valley, the city—and later the surrounding desert—flourished. By abstracting the water from so far away and diverting it to large landowners, water no longer follows the laws of nature but is subordinate to the logic of the economy. This makes Kate Ely's diagram of the hydrocycle (Figure 1.3) more representative of quite relevant realities.

Whenever the route of water is followed through from the raindrop, it always tracks back to the most powerful forces. If there is no human interference, the leaves

---

[5] Reisner, *Cadillac Desert*, p. 296.
[6] The story is also superbly told in the 1974 film noire, *Chinatown*.

of trees and of food drive the process, as transpiration pulls it up through the roots out of the soil. Whenever we get involved, it is the wealthiest who divert the water or have others to turn the taps for them. Track it and see. Sewage still flows downhill, by contrast.

Water problems are local

The biggest problem with the way that water is taught is not the diagrams themselves, but the fact that we consider water a finite resource. School teachers tell their pupils that they are 'saving' water when they turn the tap off when they brush their teeth, for instance. Parents regurgitate the message; kids generally swallow it. We forget, or are ignorant of, the fact that water that goes down the drain flows into a sewer pipe, then back into the soil or river (hopefully after being treated). Those flows then evaporate or transpirate back to the atmosphere through evaporation or evapo-transpiration and fall as rain again.

Water is better viewed as cycling than finite. How can anything that constantly cycles ever be saved, spent, or wasted? In whatever water cycles you contribute to, you are merely a temporary holding place, a minor extra in a cast of billions in a play that has been staged for as long as water has been on this planet, a single variable amongst thousands of trillions that affect the water cycle's biophysical and social processes. People and pumps can slow the cycle down or pervert it, but they cannot stop it. Turning off the tap while you brush your teeth does not 'save' water. It merely ensures that no water flows down the drain during those moments it is with you.[7]

There are consequences to forgetting that water flows around in a cycle when trying to tackle the 'global water crisis.' The idea of a global water crisis is so widespread that there are NGOs and masters courses dedicated to solving it. The idea that there is not enough water for everyone on the planet dovetails into the 1970s debates about the 'population bomb'—the limits to growth and sustainable use of 'natural resources.'[8] The debates have been renewed in water research circles through concepts such as 'peak water,' which suggests—even if the authors do not assert it—that once water is used, it is gone, just like oil.[9]

The limits of water debates are also renewed by the more recent conception of 'planetary boundaries' and the suggested limit for freshwater use of 4,000 cubic kilometres per year, beyond which unacceptable environmental change will occur.[10] Given that the finite amount of water in and around our planet cycles forever around it, however,

---

[7] There are at least three very good reasons to turn off the tap when brushing your teeth: you reduce the electricity required to pump the water to you, decrease the chemicals used to clean the water, and save money. But as you do so, please do not think you are saving water.
[8] See Sabin, *The Bet*.
[9] Gleick and Palaniappan, 'Peak water limits to freshwater withdrawal and use.'
[10] Rockström et al., 'A safe operating space for humanity.'

the concerns are more about water quality and *local* water sources drying up.[11] In this sense, suggested limits on global water use miss the smaller picture entirely but have inspired more useful conceptual work in scientific journals which relate safe boundaries with system stability and tolerable risk,[12] and we owe thanks to Professor Johan Rockström and others for sparking the debates. But the theoretical foundation that the ideas rest upon, at least for water, is shaky.

Furthermore, thinking of water in terms of finite limits keeps us locked into the 'save water at all costs' mindset, which is challenging because the logic is appealing at first glance. Intuitively, if you want more water than exists in the source you are drawing from, you should draw less water. No doubt by deciding to pump less water from an aquifer than the amount of rain that falls upon and recharges it, you are making a real move to live within the limits of that aquifer. If you use the water pulled from the aquifer to irrigate a crop, you are exposing water that was once hidden from the water cycle (in the ground) back to it. The irrigation water is then transpirated to the atmosphere through the crop's leaves, evaporated by the sun, or soaked back into the soil and possibly back into that same aquifer.

In each case, the water molecules go somewhere. Applying more water to the fields may cause more rain to fall where it is desperately wanted because more will be evapo-transpirated to accelerate the saturation rate of the clouds right above the field. But applying more water to fields may just as well cause less rain to fall if the saturation point is not quite reached and prevailing weather conditions push the clouds on. The aquifer may be recharging from the rain at a rate faster than you are pumping from it, or it may not be. Who knows? There is very little research devoted to understanding how land use affects local hydrocycles and stream flows or aquifer levels. The work adapting the concept of watersheds to evaporation and rain systems—called 'atmospheric rivers'[13] or 'precipitation-sheds' (as opposed to the land-based 'watersheds')[14]—is, in this sense, precisely the kind of science that we need.

To be clear, overpumping aquifers or polluting rivers are ruinous practices that must be stopped. Farmers from Zambia to Azerbaijan suffer the consequences first. Habitats are ruined, ecosystems destroyed, human life impoverished. The graveyard of dead water bodies includes Lake Poopó, Lake Urmia, Lake Tulare, Lake Mead, the Oglala (or Ogallala) and Ceylanpinar Aquifers, the Dead Sea—but the hundreds of thousands of lives destroyed remain anonymous. The point is that when we think water is finite, we think we must 'save' it, but, in doing so, we ascribe all sorts of ideas

---

[11] Consider taking the same thought experiment that my postgraduate students are encouraged to: What would the water cycle look like (in terms of quantity and quality) if there were more than 500 billion people on the planet? The answers always end up being about (the very serious concerns over) water pollution, or are related to timing and rates of evaporation and precipitation rather than simply about volume. Water quantity problems are local, water quality problems ubiquitous.

[12] Zipper et al., 'Integrating the water planetary boundary with water management from local to global scales.'

[13] Waliser and Guan, 'Extreme winds and precipitation during landfall of atmospheric rivers.'

[14] Keys et al., 'Analyzing precipitationsheds to understand the vulnerability of rainfall dependent regions.'

to it that are not actually useful for sustaining the water bodies that the water comes from. When it comes to water: think locally, act locally.

Scarcity is constructed

With the cycling bit of water understood, using water sustainably essentially means having sufficient water of the right quality at the right place at the right time.[15] But 'water is finite' thinking suggest sustainable water use is all about limits and scarcity. As geographer David Harvey says, 'the invocation of "limits" and "ecoscarcity" should ... make us as politically nervous as it makes us theoretically suspicious.'[16] Scepticism is warranted when 'water scarcity' is used to justify a new policy or project. Water scarcity is a scourge, we are told. Water scarcity causes conflict, and climate change is making it so much worse. When coupled to the resource-allocation mindset that we use to manage the world, scarcity is not a feature: it is only a problem. With images of parched earth in our head, we hold these ideas about scarcity very tightly: there is not enough water to meet the demand. As with many unchecked assumptions, the muddled thinking serves to legitimise certain world views and discredit others.

Consider the extent to which water scarcity (or a shortage of anything, really) is determined by needs. The precious little water in the Namib Desert does not really bother the species that have adapted to survive there. The stenocara beetle spreads its hydrophilic ('water-loving') wings to catch the fog, while the wild desert horses can go days without a drink. Camel spiders do not need to drink any water at all; they get all they need from the blood of their prey. By contrast, the extreme dryness was a real problem for the Herero people when the German colonisers forced them into the desert in 1904 and prevented their return. Four years later, up to 100,000 people had died of dehydration, and the genocide was complete. Water scarcity is not an issue if you've adapted to it; it's a killer if you have not.

Farming families feel the blunt edge when the expected rains don't come. The Dust Bowl that resulted from the severe droughts at the height of the 1930s Great Depression in the United States led to massive social upheaval. Thousands of people from Oklahoma and other prairie states retreated westward to the wetter parts of California to make another go at life. The droughts were a real problem because so many people depend on a reliable water source for their livelihoods. The Native American peoples that lived in the region before these settlers were more resilient. Their lives were not so drastically affected by the lack of rains—although water was a key part of the 'civilising' mission that either wiped them out or colonised them.

When trying to understand the implications of misunderstanding water scarcity, it is helpful to distinguish between two types of scarcity. Temporarily or permanently lacking

---

[15] See Angela Morelli TEDx Oslo talk, 21 June 2011, www.youtube.com/watch?v=p8YHa1W_neI.
[16] Harvey, *Space of Hope*, p. 217.

'enough' water is referred to as 'biophysical' water scarcity—droughts and dry spells that ruin moist societies. Experiencing biophysical scarcity is painful, and it is entirely different from the feeling of someone else depriving you of water. That is, when clean water is denied to people because of lack of money (as in Detroit, Cochabamba, or Dar es Salaam), class/caste (as in Mumbai), or nationality (as in the West Bank), this is 'social' water scarcity, a human-caused affliction that affects every corner of the globe.

The more that people need water, the scarcer it can become. Once people are dependent on a water source to the point that they need it to maintain their way of living, that scarcity bites even harder. Like fear, needs can be manufactured. With roots in the propaganda ministries of First World War states, the advertising industry knows this well.[17] Its clever messaging managed to turn women into smokers in the 1920s by suggesting they seek equality with the cigarette-toting men, thereby doubling the demand. Likewise, if nationalism can be instilled so firmly in parents' minds that they send their children into dangerous battles on other continents, it is a simple trick to get people to pay more to upgrade perfectly functional smartphones—or to create a thirst where there never was one.

There was little 'need' for water in southern California before the industrial farms were established in the Cadillac Desert, but the thirst there is insatiable now that it supplies about half of the world's almonds and pistachios. Likewise, the demand for water before the Atatürk Dam was completed on the Euphrates River in south-eastern Turkey in 1990 was a tiny fraction of what it is today—now that it supplies (with Iran) the other half of the world's almonds and pistachios. The steady source of water is common to both mega-projects because it is a necessary condition for farming corporations to take the risk, create the jobs, and collect the profits. Interests from all sectors quickly become vested. When there is land to plant crops that can be sold, the water will be found. The need for water becomes difficult to reverse, and biophysical water scarcity becomes a real risk to the business model, social water scarcity an afterthought.

When water needs and scarcity are created, however, the risks are more acutely felt by the people who never took them. The hand-to-mouth farmers at the tail end of the Euphrates in Iraq make do with the water that has not been used by all dams upstream of them (see Chapter 4). From a perspective of international relations, the more upstream water use is established, the more difficult it is for downstream water users to negotiate a fair share of the flows, and the more they suffer from social scarcity.

Rain is commodified

We are truly failing younger generations if the water cycle that we teach is misleading or forgotten or if most people think that the water crisis is global and that scarcity is

---

[17] See Adam Curtis's documentary exploring the geopolitics of messaging in *The Power of Nightmares*, Episode 1, 'Baby It's Cold Outside,' BBC, www.imdb.com/title/tt1264687/.

just about a lack of water. And we are doing an even greater disservice if we do not share how these dynamics play out within the very flexible but firm political economic system in which decisions are made and all the vested interests lie (see Chapter 2).

The ultimate result of this failing is that we stop thinking altogether about where our water comes from or where it goes. The ignorance is strongest in those of us born with the privileged and enviable position of reliably having water at our taps 24/7. We do not think about the source or fate of the water because we do not have to think about it. In Damascus, the names of the engineers who created the 1920s drinking water system from the Barada River and the Ain al-Fijah spring are engraved in the marble tiles of the French colonial palace that was built to house the administration of the system. I know of nowhere else in the world where people so appreciate those who go to such great lengths to get you safe drinking water—even going so far as to risk their lives to keep the system going when the bullets are flying (see Chapter 3).

Usually, the municipal water staff are forgotten, unacknowledged, unknown. They find you a decent source of water, pump it to a water treatment plant, filter and purify it, then pump into storage towers so that there is enough pressure for you to wash your dishes. Then they build the sewers that drain away your raw sewage and treat it at a wastewater treatment plant (through a process much more complicated than simply purifying the water at source). The entire system relies heavily on infrastructure and processes: pumps, transmission pipes, reservoirs, chemical treatment, filtering, distribution pipes, and sewage pipes—not to mention all the paperwork that goes along with informing and billing the public. If you are not quite ready to engrave their names in marble, perhaps think of them, if you please, when you flush the toilet.

The hitch is that the more secure our water supply, the more we take that supply—and water itself—for granted. The more we take water for granted, the more we leave the decisions to be made by those who conform to and excel in the dominant political and economic forces. We thereby consent to the value of water being measured solely in economic terms—like any other 'resource,' object, or commodity. The way lumber was once a tree or veal was a lamb, water was once rain. But now it is a thing that can be priced and traded on the open and highly politicised international market: a resource that is understood only so far as we need to benefit from or manipulate it. It is at this point that our thirst just cannot be quenched.

2
Insatiable Thirst

> We pumped aquifers and diverted rivers, trusting the twin lucky stars of unrestrained human expansion and endless supply. Now water tables plummet in countries harboring half the world's population. Rather grandly, we have overdrawn our accounts.
> —Barbara Kingsolver, *National Geographic Magazine*, 2010

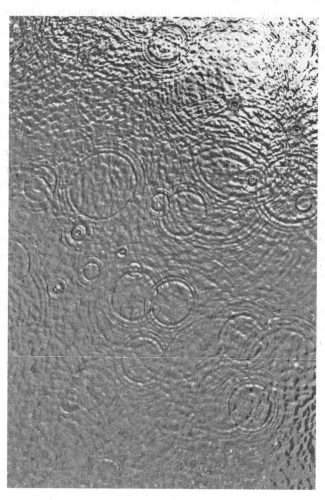

Ripples informing what is happening above as well as below the surface.

Source: Author.

The drive to satiate our thirst has driven our ingenuity in impressively clever and incredibly myopic ways. The tale of modern water delivery and use is marked by self-fulfilling ideas, infrastructure, and institutions. It is a story of nations embarking on state-size missions to extract and divert water, of winners exploiting the system, and of those who suffer whilst fighting against it. Water-saving technology has advanced so much that we can use just drops to produce crops that once required growers to divert entire streams. We can create potable water from the sea. We push water hundreds of miles across the land and up hills to those who can afford it, right past those who need it more. Even with all this know-how and capacity, water still flows uphill to money.

The resultant social water scarcity is a purely human construct. The most creative innovations came about when thirst was working against the interests of the systems we have created. But many of the 'solutions' to the challenges are devised within the mindset that created the problem. Only the ideas which develop from a brand-new perspective will get us out of our predicament, and these stem from people who help us focus on what we do with water while it's in our hands.

The mission

Hydraulic societies

All the earliest civilisations mastered irrigated agriculture, especially to grow an excess of wheat and barley, among other crops. The store of food took the pressure off hunting and allowed trade and culture to flourish. With water security, art, storytelling, exploration, religion, science, and education developed. Each civilisation then rather quickly developed the technology, practical knowledge, and policy required to sustain their ways by protecting, enhancing, or expanding their water source. In short, water spawned civilisation, which spawned the engineers and agronomists required to sustain water systems. Water creates civilisation creates water.

During the Bronze Age, Sumerian and Akkadian civilisations marshalled the benefits of the Tigris and Euphrates Rivers throughout Mesopotamia, as did the Indus Valley civilisation along the Indus River, the Ganges civilisation on the Ganges River, and the Kingdom of Egypt on the Nile. These latter were followed a few short millennia later by the thriving Nubian and Meroitic civilisations. There are also loads of smaller societies that flourished for millennia thanks to the food produced through irrigation—like the city-states around Jericho, which compete with Damascus and Muscat as the oldest cities in the world. These hydraulic societies were beyond competent as water managers. Throughout the Fertile Crescent, the first Agricultural (Neolithic) Revolution produced such a steady food supply that the societies developed cereal crops, husbandry, astronomy, mathematics—thriving for centuries more than ten millennia ago.

Before long, the institutions set up to run the irrigation systems became stacked in favour of the men who had established them and against women and marginalised people.[1] They set up sophisticated mechanisms to allocate water. Most were what are referred to as *timed systems*, in which all users would get a fixed amount of time during which they could withdraw or divert water on to their fields (rather than a fixed amount of water). This strategy was particularly effective for Oman's *aflaj* system of channels to distribute water, where the oasis-like discharge of the desert springs varies wildly from year to year.

To impose a fair structure onto the unpredictable flows, *aflaj* farmers considered plot size and position alongside the time allocations. Upstream *aflaj* users are allocated small plots, while downstream users get large plots. The upstream farmers can count on their predicted yield because they are guaranteed water whether a dry or a good year. Downstream farmers gamble more. Their plots yield less during dry years because there is not enough water to irrigate all the crops. But during good years, they harvest even more than the upstreamers. The sharing system has been codified for more than one thousand years, and the irrigation system has been functional for at least three times as long.

Apart from the music, visual art, and poetry that the secure food supply has allowed, these communities also secured supplies of milk, meat, and good relations with the goat-herding mobile communities who come in from the desert to trade. But many societies were unable to maintain their systems indefinitely and eventually dissolved. The agricultural fields in Mesopotamia became so waterlogged from all the irrigation that the soil became saline from the salts in water that did not sufficiently drain away, for example. Over generations all over the globe, people adapted by making do with lower yields or sending their children to places with more secure water sources, if they did not leave themselves. Water creates civilisation which creates water, yet water can dissolve that same society when mismanaged.

A few thousand years later, another other great hydraulic civilisation, the Roman Empire, established the means to maintain permanent locality that has, in various forms, persisted to the present. The emperors were determined to develop their urban centres and invest in their flourishing. So determined, in fact, that they figured out how to bring water from hundreds of kilometres away with minimal human or animal effort and without any electricity whatsoever.

The sole job of an aqueduct (Latin for 'water conduit') is to transport water from a clean source to the city in question, usually because the urbanites had polluted the local water source (see Figure 2.1). Because the clean water source was necessarily located at a higher position than the city, the slope of the aqueduct had to be accurately calculated and kept perfectly steady—sometimes as gentle as a one metre drop for every 5,000 travelled, for the longest ones. Whenever the topography did not follow such a steady grade, which was just about all the time in rolling hills, the top

---

[1] The command and control of irrigation systems also allowed dictatorships to flourish, according to Wittfogel's famous thesis from 1963 about 'hydraulic societies,' *Oriental Despotism*.

Figure 2.1 Aqueducts are waterways that still grace cities thousands of years after they were built, like this one built by the Roman Empire in Tarragona, Spain.
Source: Photo by François Molle from the Water Alternatives Photostock.

of the aqueduct had to be supported at the required height. The Roman engineers preferred multiple-tier arches for this because they required fewer bricks than solid walls, were more flexible (resilient to earthquakes), and allowed traffic or rivers to pass underneath.

Roman cities and citizens throughout the Empire thus enjoyed public fountains, baths, and a heightened level of hygiene. Some of the aqueducts that they established still stand today, their graceful beauty a testament to their ingenious design and solid construction. When the Empire eventually fell, the inhabitants resorted to local wells and polluted sources—and suffered through centuries of cholera and the plague.

The supply

Somewhere along this journey, our collective knowledge of the link between water and health was lost, and water was the last thing the scientific community in European capitals thought could be responsible for transmitting cholera. It was not until after hundreds of thousands of deaths, great collective misery, and a recalcitrant scientific community was overcome that the anaesthetist John Snow demonstrated the association between water and cholera transmission in London in the late 1800s. Until

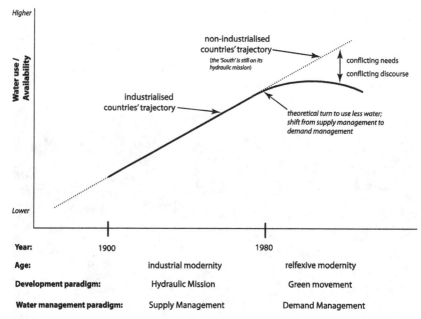

Figure 2.2 Hydraulic mission.
Source: Based on Allan (2001).

that point, everyone who was educated on the topic agreed that cholera was spread through the air, an erroneous assumption that cost hundreds of thousands of lives. By testing and tracing water sources, Snow spawned the birth of epidemiology, managed to get the local authorities to close the Broad Street Pump in Soho, and saved tens of thousands more people from the fate of urinating or defecating themselves to death.[2]

By the twentieth century, basic public health awareness and pumping technology combined with the creation and development of nation-states so thoroughly that every single modern government has sought to develop water infrastructure and institutions well beyond the wildest imaginations of the Mesopotamians, ancient Nubians, or ancient Romans. While each state has developed at a different pace, they have all followed the pattern of the 'hydraulic mission,'[3] shown in Figure 2.2. The figure shows the volume of water delivered or made available for water users on the vertical axis, plotted against time on the horizontal axis.

With the advent of petrol motors and electricity, water was liberated from the laws of nature to readily flow uphill. The impellers of modern pumps obviated the gravity-fed systems, replaced the old human- or animal-driven pumps, and made a

---

[2] See Johnson, *The Ghost Map*.
[3] Swyngedouw, 'Modernity and hybridity: Nature, regeneracionismo, and the production of the Spanish waterscape, 1890–1930'; Allan, *The Middle East Water Question*. See also Blackbourn, 'The conquest of nature: Water, landscape, and the making of modern Germany.'

straightforward task of increasing the amount of good water supplied. The heads of government and industry invested in an engineering cadre, made bold promises of 'development,' and named dams and reservoirs after themselves or the royalty who ruled over them—think Hoover Dam, Atatürk Dam, Lake Assad, Lake Nasser, etc. At some point, around the 1980s, the globalisation-driving earliest industrialised states, like the United States, Germany, and the United Kingdom, began to pump less water. This was thanks to the pressure created by early environmentalists who wanted to live within the sustainable limits of 'natural resources' rather than the scientists or politicians who followed in their wake. At least these states sought to or thought that they were using less water. In fact, they just started importing more food, so were, in effect, pumping other people's water by via food produced elsewhere. These states and the people in them are outsourcing physical water scarcity and pollution, as in the case of Peruvian asparagus that we discuss later.

States that industrialised in the decades afterwards, especially large, irrigating states like Turkey, Pakistan, and Iran, are currently following the trajectory of the hydraulic mission quite faithfully. The scene is set for a clash, then, between the people who have deluded themselves about their own state's water use and those who emulate them. Engineers or diplomats from countries that have completed their hydraulic mission suggest to their big irrigating counterparts that they start 'bending the curve' downwards, too. During the era when development funds were an effective carrot for diplomats to wave, their advice carried greater weight. But the message does not travel well today since the market of international donor assistance is so much more dynamic and the hypocrisy so much more exposed.

The infrastructure

Modern infrastructure changed the game for nation-states that embarked upon hydraulic and state-building missions. Electric-, petrol-, or diesel-driven booster and submersible pumps have radically altered the water cycle, helping liquid water defy gravity. Perhaps the best example of going the extra mile for water is Libya's 'Great Man-Made River.' The scheme abstracts water out from deep in the Nubian Sandstone Aquifer underneath the Sahara Desert and pumps it more than 700 miles to the coast through massive transmission pipes over four metres in diameter.[4] The Karakum Canal delivering water from the Amu Darya River to Ashgabat in Turkmenistan may be even longer, but Australian and American schemes for Kalgoorlie, Los Angeles, and San Diego do not trail by much.[5] Such are the lengths we go to when we have either ruined or overpumped the local water supply.

---

[4] Were water being sought to supply the demand on the Libyan coast today, the government would surely reach for desalination technology, as has every other Mediterranean government. 'Desal' has its problems, but it is a lot easier to build and maintain than a constructed river.

[5] Walton, 'Going the distance, from Ashgabat to Whyalla: 10 cities pumping water from Afa,' in *Circle of Blue*.

In terms of volume, the Swift River's redirection to Boston ranks as one of the largest transfers of water. The diverted water is stored in the Quabbin reservoir more than sixty miles away. The scheme was built in the 1920s, on land that had been taken decades earlier by European colonists who had established themselves on the territory of the Nipmuc tribe in New England ('Quabbin' means 'place of many waters' in the Nipmuc language). The downstream state of Connecticut unsuccessfully sued upstream Massachusetts soon after the reservoir was built, but they did manage to achieve a promise of a minimum flow. Like all water conflicts (see Chapter 4), the tensions are multilayered, but their histories are largely relegated to memorial plaques and information boards rusting at lonesome information centres. The colonisation, evictions and establishment of political borders that created this water conflict may not be on the minds of most Bostonians when they turn on their taps or flush their toilets. Nevertheless, the water is inextricably entwined with a messy sociopolitical history.

The great bulk of city residents around the world receive their water through similar, albeit smaller systems that include a source, transmission pipes, treatment plant, reservoir, distribution pipes, household pipes, sinks, and taps. Every part of the process is built on hydraulic missions which ranged in intensity from unenthusiastic to outright zealous.

The mission often begins with a dam. As visible expressions of economic and political power, dams are iconic symbols of the hydraulic mission. By lifting the height of the river behind them, dams can produce electricity (as the water is passed by gravity through turbines which create electricity—referred to as 'hydropower') and a secure source of water from which to irrigate. Thanks to their ability to capture the popular imagination, large dams 'offered a way to build not just irrigation and power systems, but nation-states in themselves.'[6] Soon after India's independence, the Nehru government built the dams that were meant to be the end of famines and beginning of electrification. As author and analyst Arundhati Roy points out, however, mega-project momentum has attracted so many vested interests that big dams are built for the sake of supporting the industry and have become 'monuments to corruption.'[7]

Dams also create extreme social and environmental havoc because they alter the flow of rivers and create such large reservoirs. As one would expect, building a concrete or earth wall across a river affects the speed at which the river flows, how much sediment it transports, and the temperature and quality of the water—and thus all beings that had been living there.[8] Around the world over the past century, the tens of thousands of large dams we have built have displaced tens of millions of people without their consent and often to nearby places from which they can still see their

---

[6] For more on hydro-nationalism and how water projects are linked to 'big man syndrome,' see, for Spain (Swyngedouw 1999), Egypt (Allouche 2019), Turkey (Conker 2014), Syria (Daoudy 2020), or Central Asia (Menga 2018). See also Mitchell (2002: 44); Menga (2016).

[7] Roy, *The Cost of Living*, 12.

[8] Llamosas and Sovacool, 'The future of hydropower? A systematic review of the drivers, benefits and governance dynamics of transboundary dams.'

(now submerged) homes.[9] But the rivers and people are not silenced. Not surprisingly, dams have also become the sites of struggles for social justice; many are resisted outright, sometimes successfully, but not always for very long.[10] Anti-dam efforts managed to stop the construction of the Illisu, Akosombo and Narmada dams in Turkey, Ghana, and India, respectively, but only until the governments found alternative funding sources. Dams continue to be symbols of national pride and 'development' by their leaders, like the Rogun Dam of Tajik President Rahmonor or Ethiopian Prime Minister Zenawi's Grand Ethiopian Renaissance Dam (see Box 2.1 'Dams on the Nile').[11]

The thinking behind many of those who promote dams is to replicate the hydraulic missions that wealthy and stable countries like Norway and Canada have carried out. Both states are currently doing rather well by any measure, and some of this must be due to the supply of electricity from the rivers each has tapped for more than a century. At its peak, 80 per cent of the power consumed in the province of Ontario was hydroelectric, and 240 dams produced one-third of the demand in 2021. In Norway, 98 per cent of the power is supplied by more than a thousand dams. Around the world, the same sort of schemes power schools, industries, cities, and the offices of environmental nongovernmental organisations (NGOs) whose very reason for being is to protect rivers and counter dams. As with the consultants who propose using less water to managers of countries whose hydraulic missions are in top-gear, people who argue against dams being built in countries that have not yet industrialised run the risk of imposing their will so deeply that they are unable to even contemplate the 'neo' part of neo-colonial.

In the environmentally conscious era, furthermore, hydropower is also promoted as a clean source of energy, as part of the suite of renewable energy sources required for the transition away from fossil fuels. Pro-dam lobby groups leverage the interest by issuing guidance on how dams can help to mitigate climate change and adapt to its consequences[12] and lenders like the World Bank support the renewed interest in dams through channels devoted to developing 'green growth.' Some policy-oriented climate social scientists and physical scientists are attracted by the buzz as they focus on politically acceptable ways to reduce carbon emissions so that society can carry on with the way it lives. They are largely unaware of the decades of healthy debates about the long-term destruction and conflict which dams can bring or the relative benefit of other types of renewables.[13] Distant as they are from the people most affected by the dam, their messages align with those of much more powerful actors. Thus, the quest

---

[9] The Three Gorges Dam in China displaced more than 1 million people (see, e.g., Heming, Waley, and Rees, 'Reservoir resettlement in China: Past experience and the Three Gorges Dam').
[10] See McCully, *Silenced Rivers*.
[11] Menga and Mirumachi, 'Fostering Tajik hydraulic development: Examining the role of soft power in the case of the Rogun Dam.'
[12] IHA, *Hydropower Sector Climate Resilience Guide*.
[13] See, e.g., the Riverscope method to assess impact and viability of hydropower projects. https://riverscope.org/

Box 2.1 Dams on the Nile

It is no surprise that the longest river in the world has its share of bad dams. The dam being built just after the headwaters of the Nile's eastern tributary is currently the hottest water topic about. The tensions created by Ethiopia's ongoing construction of the Grand Ethiopian Renaissance Dam (GERD) are so great, in fact, that they crowd out other news headlines—which is a very rare feat for water. And for good reason, too. The dam is designed to have the capacity to produce up to 6,000 megawatts, which would be enough to electrify the entire population of the surrounding provinces (should it be provided to them). Even before it is completed, however, the GERD has pitted people in the neighbouring Amhara and Benishangul-Gumuz regions against each other as leaders vie for power and benefits related to the dam, including more than 200 people massacred in Metekel just before Christmas in 2020.

Tensions are just as high with downstream neighbours Sudan and Egypt. Running the river through the turbines will fundamentally alter the Nile's flood-flow cycle, change the water temperature and oxygen levels, and stop the fertile silt from enriching farmer's fields and clogging up the reservoirs of dams further downstream. As such, many in neighbouring states can benefit, particularly those who are able to pay for the electricity. But many more will have to adapt, notably the Sudanese and Egyptian farmers who have grown accustomed to the pulse, quality, and character of the Nile flooding over hundreds of centuries.

The GERD has attracted loads of diplomacy, much of which reads the prevailing political winds to back the supposed winner. The Trump administration in the United States engaged fully in this mercurial 'weathervane diplomacy' when they bypassed the US State Department to fully support Egypt in 2019. Ethiopians have paid for the dam with their own hard-earned money through a tax levied by their government—even upon Ethiopian women working as wage-slave domestic servants abroad. The sense of popular ownership mixed with nationalism and ceaseless human exploitation will not be easily countered by mediators who take sides.

The GERD is just the latest in a series of dams built over the past century. The first large dams on the Nile were built in upper Egypt, at Aswan. The Aswan Low Dam was completed by the British in 1902. It was a remarkable feat, considering the absence of mechanical equipment, but 'the state must struggle, and the people must starve in order that professors may exult and that tourists find someplace to scratch their names.'[a] The first part of the Aswan High Dam was completed by the Egyptian government in 1964, and was referred to as 'Nasser's pyramids.'

The Aswan High Dam was built so far north in Egypt that its reservoir inundated a large part of Nubian territory, including in Sudan, thereby displacing more than 100,000 people and sparking the Nubian struggle for independence. The dam was designed to supply up to 2,100 megawatts of power and has enabled the electrification of thousands of villages. The dam has also deprived the downstream farmers of the fertile silt that had sustained their fields thousands of years beforehand. To maintain the yields that they are used to, many of these farmers now need to buy and apply artificial fertiliser, which brings its own set of environmental and social issues. Back upstream, the dam is immortalised by Nubian people as a tragedy; tensions remain high decades later and inform the struggles of people displaced by later dams, such as the Merowe.

The Merowe Dam exemplifies the idea of a bad dam with a bloody history. It sits well downstream of the GERD just upstream of the Aswan High Dam on the Nile's fourth cataract. Long before the dam, these were the rapids that slowed the advance of the troops of British Major Garnet Wolseley in his failed quest to rescue Major General Charles Gordon in 1898, who was beheaded at Khartoum shortly thereafter. This led to the massacre at Omdurman on the site of the confluence of the Blue Nile and the White Nile, where British troops used the world's earliest machine guns to kill more than 13,000 men from the Mehdi's army, losing only 47 of their own.

In 2009, the Merowe Dam was completed by the Sudanese Dams Implementation Unit (DIU) to produce up to 625 megawatts. The DIU had been established by and was answerable only to then-President Omar Bashir. As such, it operated above the authority of the ministries of electricity, agriculture, and water and all the skilled and dedicated technocrats therein. The construction of the dam displaced many of the residents of the dozens of riverside villages of the Hamdab, Amri, and Manasir peoples, who were forced to relocate again by the filling of the reservoir. Their protests were met by the full violent force of the armed wing of the DIU, which injured hundreds of people and killed at least one. Adding insult to injury, the President himself is said to have warned the people that they should 'flee like rats' when the gates were first closed and the water rose.[b]

The Sudanese government did offer some financial compensation to the displaced people for their lost homes and lands and provided homes in new villages with better health and education infrastructure. But the new villages were out in the middle of the desert, and the irrigation schemes upon which they were dependent largely failed after a few years.[c] Unlike the small irrigation pumps that had been adapted by and were maintained by local people, the new schemes were an order of magnitude larger and more complicated—and unreliable. Today, the resettlement villages are quiet and dim; most men have sought work in Khartoum or in the Arabian Gulf. Many who remain will tell you they long for their old villages, just as Nubian people continue to do.

The bulk of the electricity produced is still sent several hundred miles away to Port Sudan, to facilitate trade into Sudan. Downstream farmers who were not displaced by the dam have experienced a steep decline in soil fertility in less than a decade. As the dam has stopped the rich silt from flowing to their fields, they must now purchase artificial fertilisers, like the Egyptian farmers downstream of the Aswan High Dam. Back upstream, many of the Manasir people displaced by the reservoir took a cue from the experiences of those who had been displaced into the resettlement villages years

> earlier. Invoking the old Sudanese proverb 'lucky is the man who sees his friend eaten by a crocodile,' many of the Manasir have refused the government's compensation package accepted by the Hamdab and Amri villages and stayed on their lands. They are still without reliable electricity and healthcare centres, but they have adapted by practicing recession agriculture when the reservoir drops and maintained a fierce independence from a government that either overlooked or persecuted them.[d]
>
> [a] Tvedt, *The River Nile in the Age of the British*. See also Mitchell, *Rule of Experts*.
> [b] Dirar, *Valuing Property in the Manasir Communities near the Merowe Dam*.
> [c] Ahmed, *Merowe Dam in Northern Sudan: A Case of Population Displacement and Impoverishment*.
> [d] Dirar, *Valuing Property*.

to reduce carbon emissions has taken prime position over biodiversity and even over social justice, without too many people noticing, and rather perversely.

Large dams intervene quite totally in extremely complicated hydro-social systems. The risks involved are enormous, though they are borne mainly by the people who happen to live where the decision-makers site their infrastructure. The greatest concern is when the infrastructure industry runs amok or when the negative social and environmental impacts of dams outweigh the positives. Nepalese water minister Dipak Gyawali calls these kind of dams 'bad dams.'[14] 'Bad dams' contradict all the recommendations of the year 2000 report from the World Commission on Dams (WCD). Led by Khader Asmal, former ANC fighter and post-apartheid South Africa's first minister of water, the WCD recommended local community participation in planning; environmental mitigation; consideration of alternatives, including the 'do nothing' option; and equitable distribution of benefits with priority given to the people most directly affected negatively by the dam. Some dams can be for the greater good, Gyawali and many others argue, and should not be opposed out of principle.[15] But bad dams must be fought tooth and nail. Though the WCD continues to inspire informed activists, it was actively opposed by the World Bank when its 2000 report was released and it is routinely ignored by the clean, green hydropower industry today.

Lubricating colonisation

The easiest way to shed light on a contentious issue is to answer the question 'Who benefits?' (*Cui bono?*). For the topic at hand, this means suspending the assumption that the collective intention of statesmen engaged on 'hydraulic missions' is to satisfy the water needs of all citizens and instead having a closer look at which citizens gain

[14] Gyawali, *Rivers, Technology and Society*, 49.
[15] Scudder, *Large Dams*.

the most from it. Any hydraulic mission is, by definition, a political project. Political projects carried out during phases of territorial expansion are necessarily colonial, whether of the purely exploitative or takeover-settler variety. Controlling the Nile not only helped Great Britain to conquer and control Egypt, for example, but it also provided the country with decades of cheap cotton to feed mills 'back home.' Ditto for the Ganges River in India, to the point that a roughly estimated 65 per cent of the world's cotton exports by the 1880s left from Manchester ports.[16]

Hubris drove this period of European colonisation and seems to have stemmed from their ability to produce weapons that could kill from a distance (see Box 2.1). The superior capacity to finish off enemies made for one-sided battles against the people who lived on the land. This ease with which an average European could sail out to create an empire fuelled ideas that the colonisers also held intellectual and moral superiority over the people whom they killed or came to rule—including how to control rivers and what to do with them. Just as art and literature were central to the colonial project,[17] so, too, was water infrastructure and institutions.

Let us return to the Great Depression in the United States, where Franklin Delano Roosevelt's 1933 New Deal created a stunning transformation of life along the Tennessee River. Passing from Kentucky through Alabama, Mississippi, and Tennessee, the newly created Tennessee Valley Authority (TVA) had built a navigable canal and 16 hydroelectric dams by the end of World War II. Institutional history tracks the TVA as one of the most productive development projects the world had ever seen.[18] The transportation routes led to vast agricultural schemes and great volumes of food. The power that was produced supplied aluminium smelters and enabled uranium enrichment, notably for the creation of the atomic bombs that killed around 250,000 people in Japan soon afterwards.

But the TVA accomplished much more than this. The TVA also enabled and cemented American conquest of a large part of the North American continent, especially during the later stages of the incessant land- and river-driven push westwards by American and European colonials (which slowed only for a moment where the Great Plains begin, at the 100th meridian). The Tennessee River itself was in fact referred to by the earliest colonials as the Cherokee River, in recognition of one of the Native American tribes that had established itself along the river's banks and for whom the river had been a source of transportation, food, and safety from other tribes—and, for a while, from the settlers. In this sense, the food, fertilisers, weapons, aluminium, and other things that the TVA produced have proven to be either beneficial or near-genocidal to roughly equal numbers of people.[19]

---

[16] 'Manchester,' *Wikipedia*.
[17] See Said, *Culture and Imperialism*.
[18] See Delli-Pricoli, 'Participation, river basin organizations and flood management,' and Pruitt, 'Why the Tennessee Valley Authority was the New Deal's most ambitious—and controversial—program.'
[19] Move north to the Rainy Lake or the Salish Sea on the Canada–US border (Strube and Thomas, 2021; Norman, 2012) to see how other First Nations experienced much the same fate of co-colonisation by both states. See also the Decolonizing Water website.

The TVA nonetheless inspired similar development initiatives throughout the globe, not least of all along the Mekong River[20] and in Ethiopia. Ethiopia's mid-twentieth-century emperor (and Rastafarian hero) Haile Selassie might have had the more nefarious side of the hydraulic mission in mind when he visited the Tennessee Valley with President Roosevelt soon after World War II. In any case, he sought to emulate its grand designs throughout Ethiopia. Though not successful during his lifetime, Ethiopia's current dams—the Gilgel Gibe dams on the Omo River, as well as the GERD—are today's concrete expressions of that grand vision, literally and metaphorically. They also benefit the people in the political capitals more than the people they displaced, whether in Ethiopia, Tanzania, or Sudan.

The early Zionist settler-colonists of Palestine achieved a much more complete manifestation of the TVA along the West Bank of the Jordan River. In fact, the first water resources development plan of the newly created state of Israel in 1948 was called the 'TVA on the Jordan.' The plan was led by American irrigation and power engineer James Hays, who had been a project manager for the original TVA. At the outset of the plan, he wrote that 'Jewish agricultural settlements are reversing the long trend of wasteful land decline' caused by the Palestinian farmers. Carried out within the context of the British fleeing the land they occupied in Palestine and the UN's proposal to establish a Jewish state alongside an 'Arab' one, the TVA on the Jordan's main architect Walter Lowdermilk proclaimed that 'For the Jewish people this decision opens the way for the urgently needed immediate mass immigration of many, many hundreds of thousands, and—as corollary—makes particularly pressing the question of *irrigation in Palestine's southern desert*, the Negev' (emphasis added).[21]

The TVA on the Jordan plan sets out hydroelectric projects along the Jordan's Yarmouk tributary, irrigation projects in the river's upper reaches, and a canal that would take water from the Lake of Tiberias all the way to the Negev desert. Once completed, Lowdermilk proclaimed the project 'would give an example to the backward Middle East, to stimulate other and greater valley projects in Iraq, Syria, and Egypt.'[22] A similar tone is struck by the chairman of the UN Commission on Palestine Surveys when he states that the report is 'tendered with humility and esteem to the brave men and women whose labours have already done so much to make a *desert bloom* again and who are striving so nobly to build a thriving and progressive civilisation on the ruins of ancient glories' (emphasis added).[23]

Reading the original document seventy years after it was written, it is remarkable to consider how the planners' language so directly reflected their intentions. There is no hiding the assumed moral and technological superiority of the colonisers over the people who lived on the land. These assumptions were, in fact, used to promote the initiatives. Current water development projects are couched more as cooperative

---

[20] Sneddon and Nguyen, 'Politics, ecology and water: The Mekong Delta and development of the Lower Mekong Basin.'
[21] Hays, 'T.V.A. on the Jordan: Proposals for irrigation and hydro-electric development in Palestine,' x.
[22] Ibid., xiii.
[23] Ibid., xvi.

acts of goodwill.[24] Equally impressive is the extent to which the ideas became a reality. The resultant Zionist development of intensive agricultural schemes in Palestine before 1948 heaped pressure on the ruling British to accept more Jewish refugees from Europe.[25] Soon after the Palestinian Nakba, the first Israeli Prime Minister visited the TVA in Tennessee, subsequently built hydroelectric projects and canals, and the desert bloomed.[26]

In assessing the relative merits and consequences of the project, a critical mind would question whether the evidence of sophisticated and substantial water use by the Palestinians was overlooked. These farmers had been working the lands for several centuries before the Holocaust and other European and Asian attempts to exterminate Jewish people that pushed so many to Palestine. Working from within the sustainable limits of the surface water and groundwater that were available, the local people had been producing more than enough food for everyone,[27] enough Jaffa oranges to be exported to Europe.[28] A critical mind would also question the reasoning for the exclusion of Palestinians from the benefits of the Israeli hydraulic mission. But selectivity and discrimination are to be expected when water is understood to be a political tool and when politics is rife with chauvinism.

The thirst

The momentum of hydraulic missions made many of them unassailable juggernauts. The industries of engineers, construction workers, and powerful agricultural producers combined with the political class to extend water development efforts in whichever direction they were being pushed. If the thirst had been satiated in one place, the industry obliged more demand to be created, more projects to be found, more profit to be made. It was inevitable that control of the hydraulic mission would turn to the private sector at some point. The private sector created solutions that appealed to decision-makers as political economies changed. Similarly, ideas about reducing the demand for water or different ways of learning about and conceiving of it could not fit into the logic of decision-making systems. They received no serious consideration.

Instead, water and financial interests began merging. Rain formally became a commodity in 1972, when people referring to themselves as the 'global water community'

---

[24] See Zeitoun, *Power and Water*.
[25] Alatout, 'Bringing abundance into environmental politics.'
[26] Alatout, 'Towards a bio-territorial conception of power: Territory, population, and environmental narratives in Palestine and Israel.'
[27] See, e.g., Messerschmid (2008), NSU (2008), and Salman Abu Sitta's 'Atlas of Palestine '(Abu Sitta 2011). Those who are interested in the colonial records of water use and plans are also encouraged to read Saunders (1881), IRJWC (1907), Masterman (1908), Soskin (1920), Hiorth (1938), GSI (1943), and the archives of the British Commonwealth Office (CO 1938, 1927, 1926) and British Foreign and Commonwealth Office (FCO 1979).
[28] See the film *Jaffa, the Orange's Clockwork*, directed by Eyal Sivan. https://www.imdb.com/title/tt1720949/.

declared that water 'should be recognised as an economic good.'[29] During the 1992 International Conference on Water and the Environment (ICWE) in Dublin, experts from a wide variety of UN institutions established recommendations for water conservation within the mindset of water's economic value rather water as a human right. Briefly, these experts stated that (1) fresh water is a finite resource that is necessary to sustain life; (2) water management requires participation from everyone, from average users to policymakers and politicians; (3) women are essential to water management and protection; and (4) water should be recognised as an economic good.[30]

It was not long before the impact of the so-called Dublin Principles became apparent. In its wake, international development banks and private water supply companies joined to begin steering the global water community.[31] The effect has endured: getting more 'dollars per drop' is a goal in and of itself, rather than means to get better water to more people or to end poverty. Efforts to recover these costs began to trump intentions to provide quality water for everybody. Those who managed water for other people followed each trend set by the rulers of the political economic system and developed guiding paradigms accordingly: first, river management, followed by integrated water resources management, water-energy-food nexus management, and the next paradigm, which may not see water as a 'resource' at all. Each new management paradigm was progressive in the sense that it built on the failures of the previous ones. But each remained so deeply rooted to the idea that water was nothing more than a 'resource'—what Professor Jeremy Schmidt calls 'normal water'[32]—that lakes came to be seen as reservoirs, rivers became drains, and aquifers became climate change buffers. We become hostage to the way we view the world and unable to change it.

Water for the wealthy

Somewhere around the time that statesmen in the earlier developing states imagined they were on the downward trajectory of their hydraulic missions (i.e., using less water), many municipalities began selling their assets and responsibilities to private companies. The cash offered to municipalities in return for offloading creaky infrastructure and dissatisfied citizens was too big an opportunity for many of them to pass up. In response to their compatriots' concerns that they would have less control over and pay more for water, city treasurers assured concerned citizens that the private sector would deliver better water more regularly since it was ever so much more efficient. Starting around the 1980s, drinking water services were privatised

---

[29] Newton, '*Water, Water Everywhere, Nor Any Drop to Drink.*'
[30] 31 January 1992, at the International Conference on Water and the Environment (ICWE), Dublin, Ireland, organised on 26–31 January 1992.
[31] An excellent critical institutional history of water management and global governance is offered in Schmidt (2017).
[32] See Schmidt, *Water.*

throughout the United Kingdom and in a few European and North American cities. Several European water companies were given a boost by international donor agencies when the model was pushed on big cities in developing countries.

There is a strong logic which suggests that linking the private sector and water delivery or water resources management is a good thing. Any resource that 'fits' easily into the dominant economic system should thrive within the systems we have created on our planet, especially if it is considered precious. If a resource is important for the economy and can be quantified (and accounted for), it can be managed in a way that conditions it for reliable trade in markets. As a properly regulated market encourages sustainable use and equitable distribution (as economist Adam Smith's 'invisible hand'[33]), civic cohesion and the sustainability of the resource should be assured. Consider how fossil fuels have bankrolled so many state projects or how the oil industry has managed society's turn towards other sources of energy as alternatives to fossil fuels so effectively that it has not had to reduce production. The same logic suggests that water should be priced lower when it is abundant and higher when it is 'scarce.'

But water is very different from oil. Politically, fossil fuels facilitate industrial production, drive weapon systems, find their way to whomever is ready to pay, and divide nations. States will go to war to steal another's oil or gas. The fuels feed the war effort itself or can be sold to raise the funds required to perpetuate it. Water does none of this. Cycling around like a fugitive, it is often not so readily controlled. And it is not worth much on markets: the United States and United Kingdom did not invade Iraq to use the Euphrates River to grow dates (more on that in Chapter 4). Furthermore, few people have any sort of the same emotional connection with oil that so many have with water. The very strong connection that water has with life and dignity—and water's essential qualities—make of it a 'resource' like no other. Not a resource at all, in fact; water is part of us and we are part of water.

The right to water is now enshrined in General Comment 32 of the International Covenant on Economic, Social and Cultural Rights, by the UN General Assembly,[34] and in several national or subnational constitutions, as in South Africa and California.[35] Despite the fact that you would have to go to the darkest corners of our world to find someone who would willingly deprive another of enough water to drink, the human right to water is not a popular idea. A good half of global water policy influencers will openly state their opposition to the right to water or their disdain for those who fight for it. The idea that all people should have equitable access to enough safe drinking water is not helped by viewing water as a commodity. If commodifying water worked, we would expect that the poorest people pay less for water, might receive more, or perhaps receive the best quality of water.

---

[33] Smith, *Wealth of Nations*.
[34] GC15, 'Substantive issues arising in the implementation of the International Covenant on Economic, Social and Cultural Rights, general comment 15 (Draft).'
[35] McCaffrey, 'The human right to water revisited,' in *Water and International Economic Law*. de Albuquerque, *Realising the Human Rights to Water and Sanitation*.

In many well-regulated societies, cross-subsidisation of drinking water ensures that the bigger water users pay more for every cubic metre of water delivered to them. This allows those who are less able to pay to pay less. But, in far too many places, it is the poor who pay the most for water.[36] For people living in some villages on the West Bank of the Jordan River that are not served by water networks, the cost of water is up to ten times the cost paid by the residents of Ramallah or settlers in the colonies. This is because the villagers must cover the cost of delivery of the water from the spring, either by truck or donkey. The longer the carriers are held back by Israeli soldiers at checkpoints, the higher the cost.

Often, those on the margins of society are also on the physical margins of the water distribution network. If these users want clean water, they must tap into the pipes that were laid down for others. This is why there are so many honest and moral people criminalised for 'stealing' water in el Alto and Cochabamba, Bolivia; Dar es Salaam, Tanzania; Baghdad, Iraq; Mumbai, India; and too many other places. When they are prevented from illegal tapping, marginal communities fetch contaminated water from tap stands, leaks in pipes, or puddles—thereby risking severe gastrointestinal disease.

If water markets in poorly regulated societies worked, everybody in the world would have access to safe water. But this is a luxury only for about 1 billion people, while twice as many have no access to proper wastewater services.[37] Meanwhile hundreds of thousands of children die from water-related diseases that have been largely eradicated in industrialised economies.[38] The stats are so well-known that your eyes likely glaze over as you read them.

It would take about 30 billion US dollars annually to ensure availability and sustainable management of water and sanitation for all,[39] which is at the heart of the sixth of the UN's Sustainable Development Goals. It's a hefty amount, but not much more than the average European country's annual military budget. You can lay a lot of pipe with the money it costs to produce or even to fire a missile. Like education, drinking water is relatively cheap to provide and would bring so many people onto equal footing, yet we have not made the necessary decisions to suitably provide either. Ever since the 1960s, people trying to clean up water supplies have been voicing their frustration along the lines of 'We can put a man on the moon, but can't get water to every child.' Half a century later, billionaires can (and do) launch themselves into space, but we still fail to supply all kids with clean water. Water still flows uphill towards money and power. Unfortunately, sewage still follows the laws of nature and flows downhill, to the slums.

---

[36] UNESCO, *The United Nations World Water Development Report 2019*.

[37] WHO/UNICEF, 'Highlights from progress on household drinking water, sanitation and hygiene 2000-2020: Five years into the SDGs,' from Joint Monitoring Programme for Water Supply, Sanitation, and Hygiene.

[38] Prüss-Ustün et al., 'Burden of disease from inadequate water, sanitation and hygiene in low- and middle-income settings: A retrospective analysis of data from 145 countries.'

[39] Hutton and Varughese, *The Costs of Meeting the 2030 Sustinable Development Goal Targets on Drinking Water, Sanitation, and Hygiene*, ix.

In the United Kingdom, the right to safe drinking water is legally enshrined, and the private water companies cannot cut the supply to a house if the water bills are not paid. This is a fact that cash-strapped university students are always happy to learn but also a privilege that should not be taken lightly. In Detroit, the municipality itself cut off the supply to more than 6,000 residents in 2,800 households, mostly in predominantly Black neighbourhoods.[40] This happened before the nearby city of Flint was detached from Detroit's water supply and more than 100,000 people were exposed to the lead that leached in through aging pipes carrying water from the Flint River.[41]

As always, water availability depends on what we do with the water whilst it is in our hands, and is a reflection of ourselves. Thus, the quality and equity of the water service you enjoy is not determined solely by whether it is a private company or municipality that supplies it, but also by how societies set themselves up or are regulated. When they are effectively regulated, some private companies do a better job than some local governments.

Nonetheless, there are at least two good reasons to fight against the privatisation of water services or for the re-nationalisation that has occurred in Athens, Paris, Berlin, and elsewhere. The first is to keep the profits in the system. From 1991 to 2019, even as they were dumping untreated human sewage into rivers thousands of times every year, private water companies in the United Kingdom paid approximately 80 billion US dollars—not to British citizens as taxes, but to shareholders.[42] The second is accountability. When people demand a better water service, a private company can evade responsibility much more readily than can a municipality. This becomes an issue when times get tough. The local government of Mexico City, for instance, must reach further and further afield because it cannot cope with the incessantly increasing demand for water. Local authorities remained on the frontline when the taps ran dry in Taiz, Yemen, in 1997; in São Paulo, in 2014; and in Cape Town, in 2019, even as enough water was found to maintain nearby golf courses. Private companies fare less well during wartime. As we shall see, employees feel little obligation to their employer or customers, at least not enough to risk their lives. Municipal workers, by contrast, feel and act on their duty to provide water to their compatriots—often at great personal sacrifice.

From crops per drop to dollars per drop

Might Adam Smith's invisible hand guide us at least towards sustainable use of agricultural water? Probably, considering spectacular innovations in irrigation institutions and technology—like the *aflaj* systems of Omani farmers mentioned previously. Palestinian farmers in Jericho have similarly worked out a time-based allocation

---

[40] Felton, 'How Coke and Pepsi make millions from bottling tap water, as residents face shutoffs.'
[41] 'Flint water crisis,' Wikipedia.
[42] Laville, 'England's privatised water firms paid £57bn in dividends since 1991.'

system; some families have been allocated roughly 15 minutes every few days for hundreds of years, while others get more time if they bargain well enough within the hierarchy of the governing institutions. People have also developed neat technology along the Shatt al-Arab, which flows from the confluence of the Tigris and Euphrates to the sea at the Persian Gulf. Iraqi farmers around Basrah and Abu al-Khasib placed their weirs at just the right height to allow the top layer of freshwater to spill on to their fields while the heavier saltwater stays behind.

Irrigation is a bit trickier when the water is below the fields you want to quench. Along the Nile and Indus, people developed Archimedean screws, treadle pumps, or used camel power to pull the water up (Figure 2.3). In windier and flatter places like the Netherlands or east of England, the locals built windmills to pump the wetlands dry enough to be able to plant, then used some of that pumped water to irrigate. Ingenious—but devastating for all the living organisms that thrived in the wetland ecosystem (which are second in biodiversity to rainforests). Each of these systems, called *furrow irrigation*, is used to transport the water around the fields through channels.

Within the hydraulic mission, the quest to increase the efficiency of irrigation has translated into a race for ever more 'crops per drop.' From a perspective of efficiency, furrow irrigation is seen as no good because too many drops of water seep through the channels into the soil beneath. Better to line the leaky channels with concrete instead, the thinking goes. The first real wave of modern irrigation came with the enormous *pivot irrigation* setups that create eye-catching circles when seen from above.

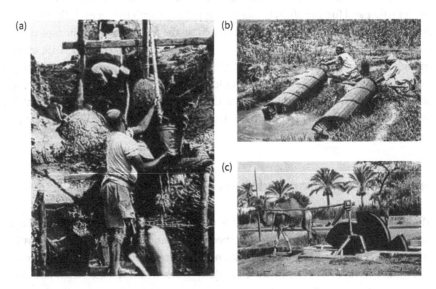

Figure 2.3 Egyptian farmers using various methods to irrigate their crops, 1945. (a) Buckets lift water by hand and with weighted levers. (b) An 'Archimedes Screw' low-lift wooden pump operated by hand. (c) Steel scoops are driven by camel.
Source: From the collection of an unknown British officer posted to Egypt

Figure 2.4 Remnants of a renewed drip irrigation system in Diama, Senegal.
Source: Jean-Yves Jamin, from Water Alternatives Photostock

But a lot of the water delivered in this way evaporates off the leaves of the plants before the roots can pull it up. Pivot irrigation has generally been displaced by *drip irrigation*, the system devised in Israel that uses small-diameter plastic pipes to deliver the required volume of water to the root structure of a crop when it is most needed. It deposits exactly the right amount of water through a small emitter at precisely the right location at just the right time.

One problem with drip irrigation is the cost of pushing the water through the pipes and filters, of replacing o-rings and lateral pipes damaged by UV light, and extra water required to flush out the salt that accumulates at the emitters (Lankford, 2018). Furthermore, when the pipes reach their end life or become clogged or outdated, there is a plastic mess to dispose of (Figure 2.4).

The much bigger issue, however, is all about the meaning of 'irrigation efficiency.'[43] In other words: Which systems deliver the most 'crops per drop'? The answer is always best answered with the hydrocycle in mind.[44] Do the old unlined furrows really 'lose' water? Or does that water just seep into the soil or aquifer, to then be 'used' by another

---

[43] The debate about irrigation efficiency may be more electrifying for water enthusiasts than for everyone else, but readers who appreciate its importance to water use are encouraged to read Lankford et al. (2020).

[44] See, e.g., van der Kooij et al., 'The efficiency of drip irrigation unpacked' and Jobbins et al., 'To what end? Drip irrigation and the water-energy-food nexus in Morocco.'

crop somewhere else some other time? It could go to another crop in the same field the next day, or much further away, but is that sufficiently efficient for farmers who rely on it? And does the water lost to evaporation from sprinkler irrigation just disappear the way you used to think the water down your sink did? Or does it form part of a cloud, and does that cloud drop more or less rain on the fields that it originated from, and is that a 'good' or a 'bad' thing? Easier to ask than to answer! The answers are quite complex, context-specific, and impossible to generalise. But some light can be shed by examining individual cases and more specific phenomena—and by reversing the question.

Desert bloom syndrome

Does drip irrigation really 'save' water? The evidence shows that, outside of the laboratory, the short answer is 'no.' To answer the question in full, you would have to consider the political and economic systems that shape the choices of the farmers and how much land is available to be planted. Because if there is demand for the crop and more land to be planted, then more water will be used. Put another way, so long as there is a market to sell the produce and land to plant in, there is a genuine risk that the water sources will be maxed out. Bob Marley saw this clearly when he sang 'When the well is full, the fool is thirsty.'[45]

The very high rate of crops per drop squeezed out for cash crops can be lucrative indeed, and the profit is too tempting to be satisfied with the levels of production that have been established. But the more crops that are planted, the more water must be abstracted regardless of how efficient the production system is. The same occurred with coal mining in the United Kingdom, which economist William Jevons explained as a paradox: technology drives efficiency of production or extraction but also demand—and therefore more, not less, is produced or consumed.[46] In the water world, the net result of the logic is a group of afflictions that social scientist François Molle calls 'desert bloom syndrome.'[47]

The syndrome afflicts the Cadillac Desert of southern California, both shores of the Jordan River Valley, the shores of the Zayandeh Rud and Lake Chad,[48] the fertile fields up and down the Mekong River, the northern parts of West Africa and the southern parts of North Africa, many coasts of Latin America, and loads of Australasia. Intensive irrigation projects exist all over the driest places on earth.

[45] Bob Marley, *Rat Race*, from the 1976 album *Rastaman Vibrations* by Bob Marley & The Wailers.
[46] See Polimen et al., *The Jevons Paradox and the Myth of Resource Efficiency Improvements*.
[47] Molle and Floch, 'The "desert bloom" syndrome: Irrigation development, politics, and ideology in the Northeast of Thailand.'
[48] Lake Chad certainly was drying up for some decades around the turn of the century, as evidenced by satellite imagery that has been reproduced so often that it is today an extremely tricky task to find out whether it is still shrinking. That is, from afar. The people who make their living from the lake know it has been increasing as upstream withdrawals have diminished. See the interesting story of how remote analysis can pervert the reality in so many remote minds in Selby, Daoust, and Hoffman, *Divided Environments*.

Insatiable Thirst 41

Figure 2.5 Asparagus growing in the desertic Ica Valley, Peru. Within the political economy which guides it, the impressively high rate of 'crops per drop' is not sustainable.
Source: Photo by Nick Hepworth, from Hepworth, Nick, Julio C. Postigo, and Bruno Güemes Delgado. 2010. 'Drop by drop: A case study of Peruvian asparagus and the impacts of the UK's water footprint.' London: Progressio, in association with Centro Peruano De Estudios Sociales, and Water Witness International.

Sprinklers in deserts, drips into the sand. The symptoms of desert bloom syndrome include all the trappings of the hydraulic mission: a generation of engineers trained to serve their governments in the conquest of nature, the widely held view that water is a commodity or a means to an end, and a flexible but firm political-economic system. Though perfectly rational from an economic perspective, the practice goes against the grain of all environmental sustainability science.

Europeans might reflect on this when they eat asparagus grown in the Ica Valley of Peru. The desert valley receives about one millimetre of rain every year but produced nearly 250 million kilogrammes of asparagus in 2008 (Figure 2.5).[49] The asparagus is conveniently wrapped in sturdy Styrofoam and cling film, delicious with garlic, and cheap, especially considering how many thousands of air and road miles it has

---

[49] Hepworth, Postigo, and Güemes Delgado, 'Drop by drop: A case study of Peruvian asparagus and the impacts of the UK's water footprint.'

travelled from the west coast of Peru. And it is lucrative—the 2008 yield was worth nearly half a billion US dollars.

The asparagus spears are produced with what is nearly the highest 'crop per drop' rate in the world through drip irrigation. Originally, the water was pumped up from the nonreplenished aquifer that underlies the valley. When the aquifer started drying up (with the water table dropping two metres every year in some places) and pumping rates became too expensive to maintain, they resorted to a new source in the headwaters of the Amazon River at High Pampas. The growers built massive concrete canals to deliver water from across the mountain ridge to the valley.[50] The alternative to diverting the river would be to work within the clearly established sustainable limits of the aquifer; that is, to produce less asparagus. But nobody has ever suggested as much. Inequalities in wage for farm hands keeps the price in Peru down and the demand in Europe high. The aquifer will remain overpumped and the rivers diverted. If the headwaters are not enough, a new source will again be sought.

In maximising the amounts of crops per drop through drip irrigation, the political economy within which the Ica Valley asparagus is grown ensures that the highest levels of dollars per drop are attained. As in many arid regions, the barren desert is transformed into a productive field. The entrepreneurs that drive the systems are like modern-day alchemists, turning water into gold. The system has failed to safeguard the environment or even share what it provides in any equitable way. Human ingenuity has managed to make the most of water as a commodity, but it has not sought to cultivate any of the cleansing, nourishing, or unifying qualities of water. This is another fact that we cannot hide from our children: we've had Mother Nature on the run for more than a century now, and the best we can do is build hyperefficient systems that benefit only those who can afford it.

Not solutions

Like someone trying to dig themselves out of quicksand, some of the ways we respond to the water issues we have created only make matters worse. Part of the reason can be attributed to the ideology of 'solutionism,' or the reductive idea that every challenge is a puzzle that has a 'solution'[51] and preferably a comprehensive one.[52] It should be clear by now that water and the way we use it are far too complex to follow any such simple and singular dogma. Dealing with the myriad of people and ecosystems and uncertainty involved obliges an approach that spans sectors and disciplines, even if this is much more difficult. But the juggernaut rolls on undaunted, and we continue to do the wrong thing incredibly well instead of the right thing somewhat clumsily.

---

[50] Ibid.
[51] Hulme, 'One Earth, many futures, no destination.'
[52] Fallon, Lankford, and Weston, 'Navigating wicked water governance in the "solutionscape" of science, policy, practice, and participation.'

Figure 2.6 'Shade balls' used to reduce evaporation and bromate levels from behind one of the dams of the Los Angeles Department of Water and Power.
Source: http://www.theguardian.com/us-news/gallery/2015/aug/11/shade-balls-reservoir-la-water-conservation-drought-california

Shade balls

Back to the Cadillac Desert: engineers of the Los Angeles Department of Water and Power (LADWP) continue to rise to challenges with the same innovative spirit that their predecessors unleashed more than a century before. Soon after the turn of this century, they found that toxic bromate was forming in the drinking water stored in their reservoirs north of the city, due to sunlight reacting with the naturally occurring bromide in the water. As they were in the middle of a drought (from 2008 to 2014, at least), the engineers were also more concerned than usual about all the water that the hot sun was pulling off the exposed surface of the reservoirs. The solution for both issues, one that had already been tested on other reservoirs, was to release nearly 100 million black plastic balls into the drink (Figure 2.6).

With the surface of the reservoir entirely covered, at a cost of 35 million US dollars, evaporation was reduced by about 1 million cubic metres,[53] thereby 'saving' enough for about 18,000 people every year.[54] Bromate levels fell to within safe levels, too, but now the quality of the water is suspected to be heavily tainted by microplastics released from the balls. This unintended effect should make us question if alternatives were sufficiently considered. What if the water were stored underground and not exposed to the sun? Could the reservoir have been designed with a smaller surface

---

[53] Clark Howard, 'Why did L.A. drop 96 million "shade balls" into its water?'
[54] That is, if you use about 150 litres of water per day at home, which is the average UK rate. The average US rate is about 350 litres, so the 'saving' enabled by the shade-balls extends to about 8,000 people.

area exposed to the sun, to minimise evaporation? Might the reservoir be covered with floating solar panels, or at least covering panels? Some LAPDW reservoirs eventually were, but the fate of the millions of plastic balls is unknown.

Another alternative that might have been considered at the time is to use less water throughout the city or the state—managing the demand instead of meeting it at any cost. Banning or encouraging limits on the irrigation of lawns and golf courses could reduce the demand in a way that may obviate the need for the balls altogether. What would be even more efficient would be to reallocate water used by the agricultural sector to consumers in the city. City residents are always ready to pay much more for drinking water than are agro-corporations, after all. This would result in an enormous hike in dollars per drop if that was the goal. With so much more water required to grow food than to drink, taking just a few Californian almond plantations out of production might help solve the evaporation problem of Los Angeles's drinking water supply.

But the interests entrenched in and profits coming out of the established industrialised agriculture systems are considerable, so this last alternative is a non-starter. Even to suggest it is to invite criticism and risk being discredited as naïve. The LADWP has no mandate to talk to the growers, and there is no reason to think that the mayor of Los Angeles would. Southern California plateaued on the curve of its hydraulic mission, and state governors have little incentive to bring it down. Even as Mexican farmers in the Baja California downstream are deprived of the flow of the Colorado River, Washington tries to ignore the international water conflict (see Chapter 4).

California's IT sector in Silicon Valley pioneered long-term sustainability of institutions through horizon scanning and 'fail fast' methods of trial and error. Critical thinking and voices abound throughout the state, from the Pacific Institute to the University of California, Santa Barbara. They spot and call out the dissonance of solutions that appear reasonable from one perspective but ludicrous from another. The issue in this case is hidden in plain sight. A city established in the middle of a desert that follows a model of barely restricted social and political growth for more than a century will always be pushing the sustainability envelope and creating tensions. The real test of our ingenuity is whether the critical voices are heard and whether we develop the flexibility required to adapt and transform some of the systems we've created.

Desalting the sea to bloom the desert

Physical water scarcity problems would vanish into thin air if we could grow food with or drink from the sea. There is so much more seawater than freshwater in the world that the supply would be limitless. Desalinating water for drinking is now so common around the world that it should probably be included in the tailored hydrocycle diagrams discussed in Chapter 1. The practice is very well established on many dry islands, certainly for tourist resorts on those islands, as one might expect. It is also established in places that have abundant water, including the United Kingdom. Tapping into the sea has the potential to become a panacea for every nation's physical water scarcity problem, to reduce the effects of mismanagement and absolve the managers.

At first, desalination appears to make little economic sense. After all, taking the water out of the sea takes a lot more energy than capturing the rain. Reverse osmosis is the most common method of desalination and is widely known as 'RO';[55] it uses filters to hold back the salts and other minerals, allowing only pure H_2O to pass. Only high-pressure pumps can force the molecules through the membranes, and every litre produced results in about two or three times as much even saltier brine.

The technology has improved by leaps and bounds over the past decades, to the point where RO requires a quarter of the energy that it once did. Depending on the price of the barrel of oil, RO is currently economically viable in many markets—at least for drinking water. If the politics add up, then the process is too tempting to turn down. A turn to desalination means that water regulators and managers do not have to confront the fact that they have failed to protect their endogenous water sources and have an option that is mostly affordable by consumers—roughly one US dollar per cubic metre.

The improvements in technology have brought the costs of desalination within the price people are willing to pay for drinking water but still far too high to produce marketable crops. It takes about one cubic metre to produce one kilogramme of carrots, which makes them a luxury once all other inputs are considered.[56] Furthermore, stripping drinking water of its minerals causes concerning health problems. Pure H_2O is the diametrical opposite of mineral water in this sense. It has none of the magnesium so essential for proper growth, especially in children. Plants need salts and minerals to grow, too—especially nitrogen. Thus, even if it was affordable, RO desalinated water is the last thing farmers would reach for.

Yet they are reaching for it in the Negev Desert. If making the desert bloom in southern Israel seemed like a good idea in the 1950s, it is because the practice was in lockstep with the foundational years of the state's early hydraulic mission. As Lowdermilk promoted in his 'TVA on the Jordan,' greening the desert was one of Israel's key foundational myths. Just as the Huleh marshes in the north were drained,[57] the Negev Desert in the south was irrigated to encourage more inward immigration of Jewish people.

Perhaps using desalination water to irrigate the desert will also come to be understood as a 'good idea at the time' or a 'mistake' fifty years hence. But, for now, it continues (Figure 2.7). By producing up to 600 million cubic metres of desalinated water

---

[55] Large-scale distillation is becoming more viable. New technology—like forward osmosis and membranes which allow some nutrients through—is in the pipeline. Ingenious stuff.
[56] 'Desal' has other drawbacks which are not discussed here. Apart from the energy required, the saltier discharge brine can ruin marine or terrestrial ecosystems—just to mention a few: see Allouche (2018) and Circle of Blue website.
[57] Yehuda Amichai, 'Once I wrote now and in other days' (2000).

Figure 2.7 Another blooming desert from a promotional poster presented at the Israel pavilion of the Sixth World Water Forum in Marseille 2012. The original title above the poster: 'Israel—63 Years of Turning Desert into Oasis.'
Source: Author.

per year (which is more than double of all Palestinian annual water consumption, including for the agricultural sector), Israel sometimes experiences gluts in water, especially during wet years, when the Lake of Tiberias is full (as in the winters of 2019–2020 and 2020–2021).[58] But the Israeli government is contractually bound to buy water from private operators exclusively and is unlikely to scale back production, even if it wanted to. Looking around, the obvious place to 'put' the water is in the agricultural sector, but farmers will not spend twice on tomatoes or potatoes which develop wholly malformed from the demineralisation. Retaining Israel's famous yields and quality of produce now requires *remineralisation* following demineralisation. The circuitous problem-solving is evidence of just how far people will go to avoid using less water.

Sugar water

Managing the demand for water is anathema to the producers who rely on using more of it. In a very real way, when Europeans eat Peruvian asparagus, Californian almonds, or Israeli potatoes, they are creating water problems for others, albeit at the prodding of the agri-business salesmen. You may have thought of the carbon footprint of eating food produced in another region of the world, but possibly not the water footprint. This is where virtual water becomes so interesting. When a dry country imports food from a wet country, it relieves its reliance on its endogenous water sources. In economic terms, this is each country making the best of its 'comparative advantage.'

---

[58] Zeitoun, Messerschmid, and Attili, 'Asymmetric abstraction and allocation: The Israeli-Palestinian water pumping record.'

Apart from putting a strain on the water of the producing nation, relying on food imports raises several other relevant questions: To what extent does importing food excuse the failings of ministries of water, for example, and avoid the crises that might otherwise lead to preventative innovation? What geopolitical concerns arise from dependence on another nation's water? In a more philosophical vein, and as hydro-political scholar Francesca Greco asked, 'What gives someone the right to eat other people's water?'[59] By considering virtual water alongside atmospheric, surface, soil, and ground water, one can begin to formulate social policy that is sustainable also for the rest of the natural world—like the Fair Water Footprints initiative which tackles the most egregious of cases.

A good example of this comes from the soft drinks industry. Sometimes the large bottlers get into trouble when they max out a local lake or aquifer at a local bottling plant, as Nestlé has in Ontario and Michigan,[60] and Coke has in Rajasthan and Uttar Pradesh.[61] Most of the time, the much greater environmental cost of fizzy drinks comes from growing the sugar required to make the syrup that is mixed with the water. Usually produced far away from the bottling plant, the effects of the sugar plantation can be as massive, though these are rarely considered. Coke has estimated the water footprint of their flagship drink to be about thirty-five litres for every half-litre bottle, depending on the growing conditions of the sugar.[62] Before making a judgement on Coke's impact on local environments or globally, one would have to determine the extent to which large-scale sugar plantations influence rainfall patterns, where the evapo-transpirated water ends up, and the extent to which the sugar crops are rainfed. Yet the company's representatives have no desire to include Coke's water footprint on its labels. 'The consumers don't need to become more confused,' was the reason give when pressed at the 2009 World Water Week in Stockholm. So, the consumers of sugar water will remain unconfused—but also unaware. Perhaps someday the labels may carry human health (such as for diabetes) and river health warnings.

Bottled water

Even more perplexing is how the same company that sells us municipal water also sells the same water wrapped in plastic. Indeed, the ingenuity which has driven innovation in bottled water should be the most sobering proof of our disconnection with the water cycle and doing the wrong thing exceedingly well. If you live in a place where the public supply is not safe, drinking bottled water is sensible. However, if tap water is safe, drinking bottled water is nonsense. If a one litre bottle of water costs one dollar in 2022, it is overpriced by *two thousand* times more than the water that

---

[59] Greco, 'Hegemony and counter-hegemony in virtual water trade: Justice for indigenous people?'
[60] Shimo, 'While Nestlé extracts millions of litres from their land, residents have no drinking water.'
[61] Zacune, 'Coca-Cola: The alternative report,' in Alternative Country Reports.
[62] Coca-Cola and The Nature Conservancy, 'Product water footprint assessments: Practical application in corporate water stewardship.'

comes from the tap. In fact, you are paying about the same for water, the 'resource' with a never-ending cycle, as you pay for petrol, the limited fossil fuel. You are paying as much for something that is delivered to your house as for a resource that states are willing to go to war over.

If your tap water comes from a series of municipal wells that tap into a coastal aquifer that is infested with seawater, nitrates, mercury, pesticides, and the like, as in Alexandria, Bangkok, Barcelona, Beirut, Gaza City, Jakarta, Ho Chi Minh, and Miami, for instance, you are doing well to secure your own supply through the private-sector options. The privately run neighbourhood-level desalination and water bottling plants fill a huge gap left by the government in such places. But if you live in New York, Manchester, Kuala Lumpur, or any other well-governed city or suburb, you are doing something entirely different, more an unchecked obsession.[63] In opting for your private financial transaction with the bottlers, you are in one sense freeing yourself from the social contract that binds you to your government through its hydraulic mission. In light of the millions of people fighting to have clean tap water in their homes, your choice is one of extreme luxury and privilege. But it does have its consequences.

Nestlé bottled water brands Perrier and San Pellegrino exemplify the trouble with bottled water. Perrier mineral water is naturally carbonated spring water that originates in France. San Pellegrino adds the carbonation to water gushing from springs in the Italian Alps. Fiji water also comes from springs in Fiji, as the name suggests (and is the 'earth's finest,' we are told). For bottled water purchasers in San Francisco, the heavy glass or light plastic bottles are shipped nearly 9,000 kilometres before the bottle even touches their lips. That is a lot of global warming for a little cooling off. Yet buying bottled water is very popular and increasingly so. Figure 2.8 shows that US citizens are drinking a lot less fizzy drinks, fruit drinks, and milk than they used to but four times more bottled water.

These buying habits also make a lot of money for Coke's shareholders. Like Nestlé's Pure Life, Pepsi's Aquafina and Coke's Dasani benefit from subsidies, as well as deception. After some negotiations with local municipalities or subnational governments, they set up shop wherever they get the most favourable financial deal. They fill their bottles from the municipal taps, give the water minimal treatment,[64] and slap on labels of clear springs and mountains that look nothing like the industrial park where the product was produced.[65] So, as you are paying exponentially more for the same stuff that comes from your tap, you are essentially buying into legalised graft.

Considering further the effort made to lay the infrastructure and institutions required to deliver safe water to our taps, our choice to drink bottled over perfectly safe tap water says something about us and our hyperdeveloped industrial societies of the 2020s. We are clearly so fraught with insecurities that we are any marketer's

---

[63] See Gleick, *Bottled and Sold*.
[64] Felton, 'How Coke and Pepsi make millions.'
[65] See 'The story of bottle water,' from the Story of Stuff series.

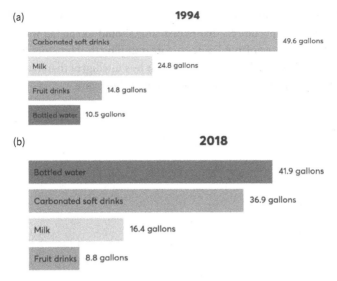

Figure 2.8 Comparison of sales of bottled water and soft drinks in the United States, 1994–2018. Soft drinks sales dropped by one-quarter; bottled water sales quadrupled.
Source: https://www.consumerreports.org/bottled-water/how-coke-and-pepsi-make-millions-from-bottling-tap-water-as-residents-face-shutoffs/

dream—we can be sold on scare tactics and conspiracies promulgating the dangers of tap water. With our and senses (and common sense) thus perverted, it does not matter in the slightest if roughly half the people blind-tested in cities throughout the world prefer the taste of tap water over bottled water.[66]

Those limits of marketing are apparently unbounded, considering the campaign run by the Volvic bottled water company and the evangelical charity World Vision. Targeting British consumers, their campaign promises that for every litre of French drinking water sold, they would provide ten times as much for 'Africa.' The poster posits a very happy (and evidently poor) teenager next to a well surrounded by dry scrub with a very satisfied (and probably English) child drinking water from a bottle in a green park. The organisations may have banked on how the campaign soothed people's consciences, but the intentions are belied by a deeply chauvinistic ideology. This dark side of water perpetuates the stereotypical image of 'Africans' as helpless or in need of our help. The incredible diversity of the African continent and ingenuity of people living throughout it is reduced to a single caricature that many of us literally buy into. Beyond the image, the marketing campaign also banks on the fact that

---

[66] Just two examples: (i) proud of the safe water they treated and produced, the employees of the water utility of German city of Duisberg tested the people of Evian, France; see Digg, 'A German waterworks marketed their bottled tap water to the French city of Evian and their reactions were priceless'; (ii) see also the spoof of glamourised bottled water served in restaurants by American comedians Penn and Teller; see Price et al., *Bullshit: Feng Shui/Bottled Water*.

we would accept an end goal of clean well water for 'African' children, which is very different from the expectations that British kids should forego tap water to continue gulping water carted over from France before dumping the container into a recycling bin. At this point, our collective water ethos is less intelligent than reactionary, more about hoarding, selfishness, and destruction than about care.

3
Killer Water

> You want it darker; we kill the flame.
> —**Leonard Cohen, 'You Want It Darker'**

Water reservoir pierced by surface-to-surface shells, Lebanon 2006.
Source: Author.

So far, we've stuck closely to the mantra 'water is life.' At the same time, we must recognise that water can be a very destructive force. Floods and tsunamis have an unparalleled ability to ruin everything we have built (and certainly deserve more treatment than this book gives them). And when society is denied water, it takes a few solid steps backwards, especially during war, when times are tough. As Palestinian poet Mahmoud Darwish recalls from the receiving end of the Israeli summer 1982 invasion of Beirut,

> The essence of war is to degrade symbols and bring human relations, space, time, and the elements back to a state of nature, making us rejoice over water gushing on the road from a broken pipe. Water under these conditions comes to us like a miracle.[1]

The return to primordialism is quicker than many would like to think. In Syria, it took only a few years before 'vicious viruses of greed, corruption, dishonesty, and ignorance had infiltrated the immune system of the communities and made clear highways for every imaginable—and sometimes unimaginable—form of torture,' in the words of architect Marwa al-Sabouni.[2] Not least of all the disease and indignity which follow cuts to clean drinking water. Thus, the rejoicing that is so visible on people's faces when their drinking water is restored to their war-torn communities runs even deeper than we think. Whenever they secure the source of water, wartime water technicians watch with quiet satisfaction as life returns to 'normal,' and people in communities begin to help rather than compete. They can at least live to fight (or take flight) another day. Just add water and watch people recover from trauma and society progress again.

A peculiar range of emotions is provoked, then, when we see water used to maim, divide, conquer, and oppress. This chapter shows how we use commodified rain to hide atrocities, clear killing fields, and force the wrong type of people out and allow the right type of people in—that is, when we are not indirectly murdering or killing people outright by blowing up water infrastructure. The unjust outcomes that stem from our water use in the political economy get even darker when considering how we use water for military tactics and violent ends.

Everlasting conflict

Water under war conditions comes not through a miracle, but through the commitment of those water technicians who repair pipes and pumps as the bullets whizz around them. With a lot of ingenuity and a bit of duct tape, a small team can keep almost any system going for some time. The reverse is also true—if key members of that team flee the fighting or are injured, killed, or retired—the taps will run dry. Employed by the municipality, the technicians are working for the people.

Sometimes wartime water technicians are pressured by their neighbours to restore the water. Other times they risk their lives out of a sense of duty to their profession, to their employer, if not to their families.[3] As the conflict drags on, however—when the bombing has stopped, restarted, died-down, and resumed—the motive for risking their lives changes. The water technicians settle into civil service mode and risk their

---

[1] Darwish, Memory for Forgetfulness, 18.
[2] al-Sabouni, The Battle for Home: The Memoir of a Syrian Architect.
[3] Personal communication with people in Brazzaville, Basra, Beirut, Jenin, and Rafah.

lives to earn the pay cheque they so desperately need to provide for their family, perhaps to send their kids to a safer place.

To understand the courageous-turned-unquestioned bravery of water workers, it helps to view armed conflict in the long term, rather than as singular events. Just consider the changes that occur as conflict endures. These include the abandonment of loyalty following the seventh or tenth shift in their leaders' alliances, the hollowing-out of ideals as the savagery of warfare can no longer be kept in check, the omnipresence of life-threatening accidents and chronic disease, and the lack of control over even the most banal and quotidian aspects of daily life. Criminals start to profit legitimately; some law-abiding citizens become criminals. Allegiances to religion, flag, or tribe are paraded about as people rediscover the identities they had been suppressing. To understand the use of water in war, you would also have to consider the fact that the suffering doesn't always end when one side claims victory.

The peace of the victors looks very different from the new reality of the defeated, particularly when the result is occupation or colonisation.[4] Consider Gaza, which Israel has alternately occupied and attacked since 1948, notably in 1956, 2002, 2008, 2012, 2014, 2018, and 2021. The months and years between the assaults are relatively calm but not exactly 'peaceful.' They are periods during which people can get back on the feet, muddle through the challenges that the rest of life throws at them, and maybe begin to think and plan a little less tactically and a bit more hopefully. But the bombs return, and they are forced to put out fires again. The people of Gaza live in the wake of the last attack and in the shadow of the next one. Friends in Iraq, Syria, and Libya voice the same sort of feelings.

War surgeon Ghassan Abu-Sitta and health anthropologist Omar Dewachi insist that protracted armed conflicts are more accurately described as 'biospheres of war,'[5] where the air is laden with disease, the water is contaminated with heavy metals from weaponry, children adapt to the fear of their parents in wholly traumatic ways, and every decision gets made in light of preparing for or evading the next round of bombing. Considered alongside the economic sanctions and trade blockades that are often placed on the losing side of a war, the biosphere of war permeates every aspect of life. A war wound becomes much more than a physical injury that is repeatedly infected: it becomes a metaphor for society—an insult and injury that tears at the interstitial tissue of community and from which it will emerge from stronger, weaker, or not at all.[6]

In this biosphere of war created during protracted armed conflicts, hospitals that have depleted their stores during the emergencies struggle to get bare necessities through the sanctions. Wastewater plants that have been damaged are patched up but later fall into disrepair. Older children wet their beds during the calm periods,

---

[4] As Lebanese historian Albert Hourani observes, 'defeat goes deeper into the human soul than victory'; in A History of the Arab Peoples, 300.
[5] Zeitoun and Abu Sitta, 'Gaza now has a toxic "biosphere of war" that no one can escape,' and Abu Sitta et al., 'Conflict medicine: A manifesto.'
[6] Dewachi, 'When wounds travel.'

54 Reflections

Figure 3.1 A reflection of a storm building out of calm in Beirut in 2019. Too many were immobilised like a deer stuck in headlights before a suite of storms hit.
Source: Author.

continuing what they started when the threats and portends of the last attack began. It is, on the whole, a deeply traumatic time compounded by water insecurity (Figure 3.1).

These in-between periods are the ripples that start before the waves on a lake, the barely perceptible but unmistakable calm before the storm. Call them anything but 'normal' or the 'rehabilitation phase,' as some bureaucrats of the paternalistic humanitarian aid industry do when they confuse the paradigms learned from recovering from natural disasters. Based on unchecked assumptions about societies recovering from war, the idea is that the humanitarian actors engage in lifesaving during the emergency, the development workers engage in 'development' afterwards, and everyone does their share. So the humanitarians risk the shrapnel to get the water pumps going, the development workers assist with the master plan to rebuild and eventually improve the drinking water system, and the former hand the baton to the latter at some point in between. But peace and war, calm and chaos, hope and despair mix so intimately in protracted armed conflicts and biospheres of war that it is never clear at what point exactly the 'humanitarians' should pull back. The bandages are pulled off a week after they are applied or fall off six months later.

Within this paradigm, water is not a source of life, nor a bubbling brook that takes the path of least resistance around obstacles. Water lubricates the war machine, is used to fulfil military objectives, and enables all manner of terrible consequences. When it is denied in these ways, water is a source of thirst and terror.

A tool of war

Of course, killing people or combatants is always just a means to another end. If the struggle is thought through properly, the goal is to win the war. Water becomes a weapon, in this case, used tactically to hide atrocities, flood enemy lines, or lure civilians into crosshairs. Water the weapon can also be used more strategically, to clear the killing fields or conquer the territory.

Hunting thirsty gazelles

The skeletons of 11 children and 6 adults were found on top of each other when diggers broke ground on a shopping centre in Norwich, UK, in 2004. Archaeologists assert that they were thrown down a well one after the other, children last, sometime around the year 1200 CE, and that most of them were Jewish. Pogroms against people of the Jewish faith were sadly commonplace in Norwich at the time, and the plaque situated unceremoniously above a fast-food court serves to remind us of a time when it was permissible, even common, to persecute and kill people based on the religion they were born into and to use water to that end.

We probably have used wells to kill people for centuries prior; we certainly have for centuries after. The bodies of 44 men were found in 119 black plastic bags in a well just outside of Guadalajara Mexico in September 2019, for instance. Apparently, the authorities only became aware of it when locals complained of the smell. 'The stench can stop you in your tracks,' said the humanitarian aid water engineer tasked to disinfect open drinking water wells in suburban yards throughout the former Yugoslavia in the late 1990s.[7] The wells needed cleaning because they were stuffed with the some of the people who previously lived in the homes. As always, it was the elders who refused to leave and sent the younger families on their way when the tanks came.

---

[7] Personal communication with water engineer, 1999.

The logic of disinfecting the wells was that a potable water supply would encourage other family members who had fled to return, to restore a semblance of normality. The engineer thought it would be a straightforward task as he sourced enough chlorine to kill everything in a large lake. The most difficult part was getting the bodies out, because the limbs kept ripping from the torso.[8] He and his team devised larger hooks that were adapted to bring the bodies up whole, or nearly whole. The innovation allowed them to clear entire neighbourhoods in just weeks and the city in a half a year. The residents eventually returned, though the memories never left.

Rivers are just as popular a place to hide bodies, though probably much less effective. King Darius made several Persian rivers 'run red,' just as Genghis Khan, Cortez, and British and German soldiers have. The dozens of young men dumped off a bridge into the Aleppo River in Syria in 2013 had their hands tied behind their backs. The act provided proof not just of execution but also of the killers' hope that their victims would not be found. Similarly, those who were dumped into the nearby Al Assi River at Homs in 2015 had been blindfolded. Shielding the victims was an act of relative mercy, but it nonetheless forced the victims' families to peer underneath the cloth if they were to secure identification and report back to their families.

The killers in Syria were neither the first nor the last to wrongly assume that a river would wash away their act. Five decades earlier, police in Paris threw dozens of Algerian people they had massacred into the Seine when they claimed for their rights in 1961. Six decades before that, the British gunned down more than 10,000 locals in Omdurman in 1898 (recall Box 2.1, 'Dams on the Nile'). More recently, the Sudanese authorities tossed more than 40 bodies into the very same confluence of the Blue and White Niles in their failed bid to stop the political revolution of February 2019. The people had been protesting peacefully before the military invaded their camp, shot, and disposed of them. At least the fate of these victims led to progress. Often, water-washed deaths are small, futile episodes in longer wars; the rivers just keep flowing through, waiting for our humanity to return.

Rivers are probably more useful to gain a military edge in battle than to obscure brutality. The Third Crusade to take over Jerusalem was halted, for example, when Holy Roman Emperor Frederick Barbarossa drowned while crossing the River Göksu in Armenia.[9] Leonardo Da Vinci saw the merits of rivers when he worked with Machiavelli and the Florentines to divert the Arno away from Pisa in the early 1500s.

The trench warfare of World War I was also a muddy mess. The terror experienced by the teenagers along the flat lands that make the floodplain of the Yser River in Belgium turned to misery when they were infected by dysentery or cholera or the Great Influenza pandemic of 1918, all of which are water-related diseases. Still, their generals shouted, 'Over the top!' The same topography also gave an edge to those defending the German invasion. With the knowledge and support of local farmers, the defending Belgian soldiers were able to manipulate the weirs and dikes in such a

---

[8] Ibid.
[9] Nicolson, 'Water in medieval warfare,' in A History of Water Series II, Volume 3: Water, Geopolitics, and the New World Order.

way as to keep their trenches dry and to flood their enemies'. The tactic successfully halted the invasion, even if the war took a different turn thereafter.

It is no coincidence that the engineers who designed the first armoured fighting vehicles called them 'tanks'. Keen to conceal their development of the devastating weapon that ultimately changed the course of World War I, the builders were told to refer to them in a way that no one would ever question—like 'water tanks', because these square reservoirs were so common to the trenches. In any event, rivers lost much of their tactical value during World War II, due mainly to the advent of war planes. But the dams along them were still worth something; at least so hoped the engineers of the British Royal Air Force. Destruction of German dams would dampen the electricity supply to downstream industry and cities, the thinking went, and these might also be partially flooded out by the release of a wall of water. This was the result, more or less, along the Ruhr and Möhne Rivers, where the busted dams led to the destruction of more than 100 factories and nearly 1,000 homes. More than 1,000 people were killed, too—mostly Soviet prisoners of war that the Nazis had conscripted to work in the industries. Nearly half were women. Today's British recounts of their heroism and ingenuity gloss over the human cost of their victory.[10]

Within decades, 'meteorological warfare' had gathered a full head of steam, as the US Central Intelligence Agency (CIA) harnessed cloud-seeding technology to make it rain and flood out Buddhist monks protesting the US invasion of Vietnam.[11] The US Air Force soon followed suit, trying to hasten and extend the monsoon season. The efforts mostly failed, and the United States fled Vietnam. But the contemplation that states could influence weather patterns alarmed the world and led to the 1978 Convention on the Prohibition of Military or Any Other Hostile Use of Environmental Techniques.[12] In effect, this was the precursor of efforts to demilitarise nature. In 2021, more than forty years after the convention, proposals to stop 'ecocide' are winding their way through the convention-forming process at the UN General Assembly and based on draft legal principles related to the environment that were adopted by the International Law Commission in 2019.[13]

Drinking water sources, if not quite rivers, retain considerable tactical military value to this day, just as they did when Flemish forces used ditches to protect their troops from the French in 1302.[14] Likewise, the German army cut off the water supply to residents of besieged Leningrad in the 1940s, and the Ukrainian army cut the Soviet-era canal supplying Crimea when Russia annexed it in 2014. Water infrastructure and sources were targeted throughout Syria at around the same time, such that families were risking their lives to get water from whatever pipe, orifice, or puddle they could find.[15]

---

[10] As in the Michael Anderson (1955) movie The Dam Busters.
[11] Redniss, Thunder and Lightning.
[12] UN Office for Disarmament Affairs, Convention on the Prohibition of Military or Any Other Hostile Use of Environmental Modification Techniques (ENMOD).
[13] Higgins, Short, and South, 'Protecting the planet: a proposal for a law of ecocide.'
[14] Nicolson, 'Water in medieval warfare.'
[15] Daoudy, The Origins of the Syrian Conflict.

Under these conditions, many have demonstrated the lengths they will go to in their search for water to bring to their families. The gloomy side here is that snipers know this, too. Sarajevo is the iconic example of a most bone-chilling tactic. In the 1990s, the snipers sat several floors up in abandoned buildings, perched like storks over 'Sniper's Alley' and waited. With the only clean drinking water source located on the wrong side of the alley, the men took their chances first. Hundreds suffered face-destroying blasts or paralysing back injuries if their heads and shoulders were not shielded from the line of fire. Desperately hoping that the hunters would follow some sort of moral code, the women of the household were sent to fetch water. When they were shot down, the pregnant women ventured out. Those who could afford it would send out others who desperately needed the cash.

Thus, people turn on themselves in the cruel biosphere of war, when cowardly men use water and their skills to kill the desperate from so far away. Darwish captures the cruelty well when describing the atrocities committed by the right-wing Christian militias at the Beirut camp of Tel al-Zaatar in 1976, where 'the killers used to hunt Palestinian women at the spring, at the broken water pipe, as if hunting thirsty gazelles. Killer water. Water mixed with the blood of the thirsty who risked their lives for a cup of it.'[16]

Clearing the killing fields

The destruction of water reservoirs throughout southern Lebanon occurred during the 2006 'Summer War,' which was launched by Israel following Hezbollah's kidnapping of three Israeli soldiers stationed at the border. The fighting was intense and asymmetrical, centred primarily on the villages of southern Lebanon and the southern suburbs of Beirut. Thirty-three days later, more than 1,100 Lebanese and 40 Israeli citizens were dead, much of the public transportation and energy infrastructure of Lebanon was destroyed, and more than a million people were displaced.

Drinking water infrastructure was not spared by the Israeli army's surface-to-surface and air-to-surface missiles. The destruction was well-documented by the array of humanitarian actors who rushed to keep the water flowing (Oxfam, ICRC, Première Urgence, Care, UNICEF, etc.): hundreds of kilometres of water transmission lines, thousands of kilometres of distribution lines, most of the high- and low-voltage electrical power lines and many of the transformers that fed the deep boreholes, hundreds of electrical generators that were readied to backup interrupted state electricity, tens of thousands of rooftop reservoirs, and at least fifty-five of the public water reservoirs.[17]

---

[16] Darwish, 28.

[17] Zeitoun, Eid-Sabbagh, and Loveless, 'The analytical framework of water and armed conflict: a focus on the 2006 Summer War between Israel and Lebanon.'

Reservoirs ensure that water continues to be supplied to homes, providing a buffer supply in the event that the source is temporarily unavailable. Perched high on hills or on legs, the reservoirs also use gravity to ensure enough pressure to get the water to the taps and, in the case of Lebanon, to the rooftop reservoirs of the commonplace three- or four-story apartment blocks. But it is a vulnerable system. Even if the pumps were still functional and the rooftop reservoirs intact, most people were without water when the public reservoirs were hit because the entire system ran dry.

By considering the nature of the damage, the tactics of the use of water in war become clear. Some reservoirs were damaged by the darts of cluster bombs, light- and heavy-gauge machine gun bullets, shrapnel from exploding missiles, or debris from the nearby factories, homes, and schools that were being targeted. Basic structural engineering forensics would assess some of the damage as 'collateral' or 'incidental' (a term used by war lawyers) because the object suffering the damage was not directly targeted.[18] That is not to discount the disruption caused by the damage—the label does not reflect the victims' suffering. Other reservoirs suffered damage that appeared more intentional, with attacks in the form of tank shells piercing reservoirs and, in a few cases, through aircraft-fired missiles. This was especially the case on the border villages, some of which had all of their reservoirs severely damaged (see Figure 3.2).

People who fled the villages during the fighting did so not because of the lack of water, but to shelter their families from the clear and present danger.[19] When asked why they did not return to their villages during lulls in the fighting, however, many named the lack of water as the reason. Only the combatants and elders did not flee, the latter out of a rugged stubbornness and desire to die in their village.

Ethnic cleansing

Especially when a conflict is protracted, water can also be used much more strategically—to take over the land. As control over the Nile River or Tennessee Valley enabled the colonisation of Egypt and America, so control over the groundwater in the West Bank enabled conquest there, even beyond the colonisation of Palestine in 1948. While the Palestinians whose families have resided in the West Bank for hundreds of years usually live in towns or villages near a spring at the foot of a hill, the newly arriving Israeli settlers colonise the unpopulated higher ground. The first thing the Israeli government lays down for them are electrical and water lines.

The settlers manage very well from within the political agreement known as 'Oslo II,' which was negotiated by the government of Israel and the Palestine Liberation Organisation in 1995. The sides agreed then that the bulk of territory in the West Bank, including most of the rural areas and nearly all the Jordan River Valley, would remain under Israeli control. The Oslo II Agreement also divided up the transboundary waters

---

[18] After the 'forensic architecture' work of Eyal Weizman, The Least of All Possible Evils.
[19] Personal communication with civilians affected by the conflict, 2006.

Figure 3.2 Public water reservoir damaged by fighting in Chama'a in southern Lebanon, 2006.
Source: Author.

as if between two states: roughly 90 per cent for Israel and 10 per cent for what many hoped would become 'Palestine'.[20] With hindsight, we find that the early cynical analysts proved to be the sharpest of all. Edward Said, for example, called the agreement an instrument of surrender—like a Palestinian version of the Versailles Treaty—and designed to prevent Palestinian self-determination.[21] Political scientist Norman Finkelstein understood the agreement as an instrument of control, one that would create islands of Palestinian self-rule or the equivalent of South Africa's early apartheid-era 'Bantustans'.[22] Referring to the agreed asymmetry in the distribution of water in particular, Noam Chomsky had said of the water elements of the Oslo I Agreement that 'The outcome of cooperation between an elephant and a fly is not hard to predict.'[23]

The intellectuals' analysis did nothing to stop two generations of Palestinians from attempting to build their state. The newly created Palestinian Authority created a

---

[20] Clot, Il n'y aura pas d'état Palestinien: Journal d'un négociateur en Palestine.
[21] Said, 'The Morning After'.
[22] Finkelstein, Image and Reality of the Israel-Palestine Conflict.
[23] Chomsky, 'The Israel–Arafat Agreement'.

Palestinian Water Authority (PWA) which embarked on its own hydraulic mission from 1995, with intermittent financial support of the United States, France, Germany, and the like. The PWA set out to build dozens of wells, reservoirs, and large transmission lines that would bring water to the people in hundreds of villages throughout the West Bank that were not connected to a drinking water network. They also developed the bureaucracy, law, rules, and regulations that befit all modern command-and-control types of water resource managers. Mostly, though, the PWA encountered obstacles.

Some of the obstacles were partly technical. Permitted by the Oslo II Agreement to abstract groundwater only in specific areas of the West Bank, the water managers were obliged to dig wells that are deeper than almost any other in the world, surpassed only by those dug to feed former President Ghaddafi's Great Man-Made River in the late 1990s. A well just outside Jenin, for instance, taps through the limestone aquifer to a depth of more than 750 metres (with the dynamic water level found around 500 metres down). But water did not gush out of the hole in the limestone for long before the submersible pumps supplied by USAID failed. Pushing water over half a kilometre upwards is no small feat and was clearly too much for both the kit that was installed and the very highly skilled and sincere US technicians who had installed and tried to fix it.

The same fate befell many of the boreholes dug in the Eastern Aquifer in and around Hebron. Drilling so deep for water might be worth the effort if there is no alternative. But it is an absurd thing to do when much better water is already being pumped from a water table that is only one hundred metres deep, only a few kilometres away. The Oslo II Agreement classes the water in that aquifer for use by Israel only, however, even if most of the water in it falls as rain in the West Bank.

These kinds of political obstacles are entirely more formidable than the technical or military ones because they are governed by the Joint Water Committee (JWC). The JWC is seen as either a very effective or severely disabling offspring of the Oslo Agreement, depending on what one wants to see done with water. The JWC is effective insofar as it slowed down and complicated Palestinian efforts to get water to the people. It may have been widely hailed as a great example of cooperation between Palestinians and Israelis by outsiders but not by those who have worked within it.

The JWC can issue or deny permits for all water infrastructure in the West Bank, be it for Palestinian villages or Israeli settlements. If Palestinians want a well drilled in one of the permitted aquifers, they must get Israeli technical, military, and political approval. If Israel wants to build or extend a water transmission line to a new settlement, they must get Palestinian approval. Sounds fair, but the Palestinians are not positioned to stand up to the horse-trading that was soon established. If they block Israeli projects to settlements that the Palestinians (and most of the international community) deem illegitimate, it comes at a cost of Israel denying their own applications for water projects in the West Bank.

As a World Bank report notes, '[T]he JWC does not function as a "joint" water resource governance institution because of fundamental asymmetries—of power, of capacity, of information, of interests—that prevent the development of a consensual approach to resolving water management conflicts.'[24] Considering that nearly three-quarters of a million Israelis have settled in 250 colonies over time, professor Jan Selby lays out the consequences much more starkly: the JWC 'enabled Israel to compel the [Palestinian Authority] to assent to its own colonisation,'[25] which means that the JWC is very effective if your goal is to replace one population with another.[26]

A target of war

Counting bodies has been the main measure of the impact of war for as long as they have littered battlefields (and wells and rivers). Yet the effects of explosive weapons are known to reverberate for months or decades after detonation and well beyond the immediate vicinity of the blast. Those who survive usually must cope with a severely compromised water service. Indeed, the violence we inflict on water systems is just as dark as the way we use water tactically or strategically to violent ends.

Generally, people living in cities are much less resilient and capable than the ones living in rural areas; few city dwellers even know the main source their water comes from. When the taps run dry, most people do not have a clue why. It could be because the water reservoir has been pierced, or the pumps at the water treatment plant have been shot up, and there's too much fighting at that moment for the repair crew to risk an emergency repair. Or, after long and protracted conflicts, that no spare parts are available and routine maintenance is no longer carried out (Figure 3.3). To get safe water to your tap, the water engineers also need machinery, fuel, and chlorine—and violence can interrupt all of these.

Cumulative impact

A side effect of this intense interconnectivity is that an attack which damages part of a water service impacts well beyond the blast zone. Like the tornado caused by the

---

[24] World Bank, 'West Bank and Gaza: Assessment of Restrictions on Palestinian Water Sector Development Sector Note April 2009,' in Middle East and North Africa Region - Sustainable Development. Report No. 47657-GZ, ix.

[25] Selby, 'Cooperation, domination and colonisation: The Israeli-Palestinian Joint Water Committee,' 23.

[26] It is much less important, but still must be said, that the performance of the JWC and lifting the thin veil which covers the Palestinian State also exposes the problems with analysis and development projects that are insufficiently critical. If these were simply irrelevant, they could be ignored. But those at the centre of the Palestinian–Israeli Oslo water negotiations experience recount how the unqualified cheerleading of Palestinian–Israeli water cooperation and acquiescence to the norms established by the Oslo Agreement diverted attention and efforts away from what was actually happening. The 20/20 hindsight shows that control of the flows has played its part in the conquest of the West Bank. A handful of those who helped from the late 1990s onwards to develop or write about the development of the Palestinian water sector have acknowledged the role they may have played in the colonisation. Most others, especially the expatriates who have moved on to other contexts, take full advantage of their privilege by not looking behind them. (Personal communication with various development workers, 2000–2021.)

Figure 3.3 Raw sewage percolating beside a home, Rafah, Gaza, 2003. A serious health hazard resulting from protracted armed conflict and economic sanctions.
Source: Author.

flap of the proverbial and distant butterfly's wings, the reach of the consequences of an explosion is almost without limit. Water services are integrated into other services; their proper functioning depends entirely on a reliable electricity supply, for example, just as hospitals and the health system in general rely on both. Knock out an electrical transmission line—often deemed a legitimate military target in the Rules of War—and there is no water at your tap. If there is no water at your tap, there is likely no water to sterilise surgical equipment at the hospital. Problems grow exponentially, jeopardising lives as much as the bombs. To carry the above example to the extreme, the shrapnel that disrupts the energy supply can shut off water supplies, which can lead to the shutdown of a factory, which can lead to a lack of jobs, which can cause mental health issues which may further affect the economy and contribute to mass migration, political tension—and maybe the conflict that started the violence in the first place.

Disastrous consequences cannot simply be attributed to the shrapnel because there are so many other factors to consider. But it is entirely reasonable to assert that an attack on a water system can lead to lethal outbreaks of cholera, diarrhoea, or dysentery. It all starts with the direct impact of the explosion. When a fighter jet fires a missile into a water or wastewater treatment plant, it can blow out the stock room, puncture the holding tanks, send shards of steel into the electrical control panels, into the motors of the pumps, or into the water workers who operate the plant. This is what happened when NATO forces bombed one of the pumping stations of Libya's Great Man-Made River in 2011.[27]

This kind of direct impact receives most of the media spotlight that is shone on the impact of war on infrastructure, probably because it is visible and can be photographed. Twisted rebar and pock-mark patterns from bullets convey the harrowing realities of war rather well. By the same token, direct damage is also relatively easy to mend—and seasoned municipal crews set out immediately to repair it. Reservoirs get patched, pumps replaced, and chlorine stocks replenished. At least for the first few turns around the cycle, in a protracted conflict.

But there is a much more insidious type of damage which deserves a greater share of our attention: that which is experienced or manifests itself indirectly[28]: the effect of water workers not showing up for work—out of fear of being kidnapped, as in Baghdad in 2004, for instance.[29] Conflict can drive people into urban areas to mix with people infected with different strains of whichever disease are present there—especially if the water and wastewater systems are already under strain or likely to cross-contaminate each other. Or when the fighting interrupts vaccination, antibiotic stewardship, or other sensible prevention programmes.

Indirect damage is trickier to identify and much more difficult to deal with than pierced water reservoirs. Sometimes it is an unintended consequence of clever coping mechanisms. Like the small booster pumps installed at the base of tall apartment buildings to suck water from the public distribution pipes.[30] Brilliant when all is done correctly, but if the public pipes are laid in ground contaminated by, say, human faeces, it can be fatal. The negative pressure induced by the household booster pumps sucks up all liquids surrounding the pipe before sending the toxic brew up to the rooftop reservoir. Consumers rarely become aware they are drinking water contaminated with other people's sewage before it's too late.

But it gets worse. As the conflict drags on, the direct and indirect impact begin to accumulate, and the corrosive biosphere of war starts to thrive. This happened in Basra, Iraq, whose residents enjoyed top-quality drinking water service in 1990 but were dying of cholera and other waterborne disease by 2015 and taking to the streets in protest about it by in 2018. The decline of the service from world-class to worst-class is well-documented and a result of the 2003–2014 US–UK occupation, which

---

[27] Part of a pattern identified and documented by water engineers based on the mess they had to clean up in Huambo (in 1985), Port-au-Prince (1985), Beirut (1989), Monrovia (1999), Mogadishu (1991), Baghdad (1991, 2003), Dushanbe (1992), Kigali (1994), Sarajevo (1992), Aden (1994, 2018), Grozny (1995), Novi Sad (1999), Dilli (1999), Southern Lebanon (2006), Donbass (2014), Kabul (repeatedly), and Gaza (repeatedly). (Nembrini 1995, 1994, 2001a, 2002, 2000, 2001b, 2010; Nembrini et al. 2003; Nembrini et al. 2002; Nembrini et al. 2001; Pinera 2011; Pinera and Reed 2009; Pinera and Rudge 2005).

[28] ICRC, Urban Services During Protracted Armed Conflict.

[29] Penhaul et al., 'American among 6 kidnapped in Baghdad.'

[30] WICRC, 'Compilation report from Wat-San activities in Iraq.'

came on the back of failed UN sanctions and Iraqi government neglect that crippled the services.[31] Several vulnerabilities were introduced into the service, as chlorine and alum stocks were depleted and many key staff retired over the decades.

Anyone who has tried to keep an infrastructure system going following repeated setbacks knows that it is like whipping a dead horse to win a race. Repairing the reservoirs, tinkering with the pumps, forcing parts that were not made to measure to fit, patching up the pipes, concocting homemade chlorine, etc. spirals into a vicious cycle as the jury-rigged 'fixes' inevitably fail. All of this leads to a point where a return to prewar conditions is no longer conceivable. At some point, every pipe repaired and each bolt replaced are nothing more than stopgaps, dangerous coping mechanisms to fill the vacuum. Water engineers describe the feeling of being like doctors applying Band-Aids to a patient suffering from severe internal bleeding. No amount of emergency funds can help, no amount of effort can stem the ensuing public health hazard.

Spreading disease

More research is desperately needed on the impact of war on water and public health. We do not yet know enough, and much of what we do know is difficult to prove. But we do know some things very well, like the role of water in the transmission of disease. The greatest concern is when the nasty bugs in wastewater contaminate drinking water. The early influenza pandemic (referred to xenophobically as 'Spanish flu') that developed through the mud and faeces that lined the trenches of World War I and spread to communities throughout Europe is considered to have killed more people than both world wars combined, for example. The lack of clean water and hygiene in the refugee camps of the Democratic Republic of Congo is blamed for the epidemics of dysentery and cholera which claimed more than 40,000 people from Rwanda in 1994 and affected thousands in Basra in 2018.[32]

In fact, the transmission of cholera was linked to water more than a century earlier, through anaesthetist John Snow's efforts to contain the spread in London's Soho district. Cholera had killed hundreds of thousands of people in England in five bouts during the previous century.[33] Rather frightfully, as well: patients shed all the liquids they have through diarrhoea and quickly become dehydrated—you can tell by the sunken eyes and wrinkly skin. Convinced that cholera was spread through the air, the medical establishment did its best to undermine Snow's rebellious and relentless sampling of drinking water from urban pumps. He kept at it, nonetheless, and the study of the ways that bacteria and viruses travel—epidemiology—was born. Chlorine was quickly found to be the best way to kill cholera pathogens in water, and chlorine treatment is prevalent in every city in the world today.

---

[31] Zeitoun et al., 'Urban warfare ecology: A study of water supply in Basrah.'
[32] World Health Organisation (WHO), 'Cholera-Iraq' and UNICEF, 'Yemen: Attacks on water facilities, civilian infrastructure, breach 'basic laws of war' says UNICEF.'
[33] Johnson, The Ghost Map.

More classical diarrhoea is also passed through sewage, and it is just as deadly: the World Health Organisation (WHO) estimates that it caused more than 1.5 million deaths of children in low- or middle-income countries, though not all cases are due to war.[34] The point being made is that how these waterborne diseases travel is, by now, very well known. As so many 'faeces-to-faces' diagrams show, the cross-contamination of wastewater and drinking water is in fact just one of several potential routes. Interrupting the transmission routes is quite easy.[35] Along with a dose of chlorine, all you really need to do is to keep water away from wastewater, as most cities in the world have managed to varying degrees. During war, drinking water and untreated wastewater systems are often crossed or re-crossed, as in the example of the household booster pump discussed above or when a wastewater treatment plant stops operating and raw sewage starts spilling out into the streets.

Back to Basra, then, where the wastewater treatment plant that was nearly complete in 1989 was abandoned by the contractors who fled the US–Iraqi fighting following Iraq's invasion of Kuwait. Pumping stations had to lift the untreated sewage from the hospitals and city centre out to the treatment plant some ten miles away on the edge of the desert, far from most people. But the pumps failed, the sewage lines filled, the stations overflowed, and raw household and hospital waste flowed onto the streets where children continued to play (Figure 3.4).

Crews were obliged to wade through the sewage to get the pumps working again, but, as the plant itself was not operational, the sewage just collected as a large lake in the sand. It was an entirely toxic brew that attracted birds and, through evaporation, created tons of salt. The birds attracted those who hunt with falcons, but the salt attracted the poor. These latter would then sell it on the market in Basra. Thus, a failed world-class wastewater system mutated, feeding off and reproducing itself in sinister ways.

But it is not possible to attribute the symptoms of an ill five-year-old to the effects of war on the sewage system. After all, they could just as well be the victim of exposure to depleted uranium, malnutrition, or any number of risks that are so prevalent in Basra. Indeed, the bulk of investigations into war-water-health remain associative. The hepatitis A outbreak during the war in Bosnia in 1994 was attributed—in part—to the virtual collapse of the water and wastewater system and was followed by 'staggering' rates of diarrhoea and dysentery.[36] Similarly, more than three-quarters of the 50,000 deaths after the sudden influx of 800,000 refugees from Rwanda in the Democratic Republic of Congo in 1994 were attributed to shigella or cholera.[37] And while there

---

[34] World Health Organisation (WHO), 'Guidelines on sanitation and health,' and 'Global progress report on water, sanitation and hygiene in health care facilities: fundamentals first.' See also Hunter et al., 'Estimating the impact on health of poor reliability of drinking water interventions in developing countries,' and Hunter et al., 'Water supply and health.'
[35] Fewtrell et al., 'Water, sanitation, and hygiene interventions to reduce diarrhoea in less developed countries: a systematic review and meta-analysis.'
[36] Mann, 'Bosnia: The war against public health.'
[37] Goma Epidemiology Group, 'Public health impact of Rwandan refugee crisis: what happened in Goma, Zaire, in July, 1994?' and Ramesh et al., 'Evidence on the effectiveness of Water, Sanitation, and Hygiene (WASH) interventions on health outcomes in humanitarian crises: A systematic review.'

Figure 3.4 Children playing in streets laced with untreated wastewater, Basrah, 2000.
Source: Author.

is clear association between bouts of armed conflict, damage to water and wastewater systems, and spikes in diarrhoea in Aleppo and Idlib, Syria, 'multiple confounders' mean that even the most intrepid and risk-taking of epidemiologists hesitate to draw a direct co-relation.[38]

There are never quite enough data to support what everybody knows. But there's a trick to watch out for here. If you hear someone making the point that it is not possible to prove that an airstrike will cause an outbreak of disease, you could accept the veracity of the assertion. But you should question their motives. They might be a scientist seeking to alleviate the effects of war by improving the common knowledge base or one hiding behind unquestioned impartiality and unchecked faith in the scientific method. They might just as well be a pilot or soldier tasked by their commander to conduct a war in a city, or an army lawyer interpreting the Rules of War in a way that allows military objectives to be met with more, not less, collateral damage. The former is simply following orders, while the latter is actively and creatively legitimising suffering.

---

[38] Abbara et al., 'Weaponizing water as an instrument of war: diarrhoeal disease and the Syrian conflict.'

Toxic biospheres of war

The worst outbreaks of cholera globally this century have occurred in Yemen. More than 2 million cases and 3,500 deaths were reported in 2016 and 2017, thought to be due in large part to battle damage of water and wastewater services.[39] The country does not have a lot of water to draw on in the first place, with coastal cities suffering from saltwater intrusion and even Ta'iz famously running out of drinking water in 1996. Only about half of the people in the country had access to safe piped water services.

By 2019, more than 145 airstrikes on water and wastewater facilities in Yemen had been recorded.[40] By 2020, ten of the country's thirty-three water treatment plants and five of the country's twelve wastewater treatment plants had been damaged or destroyed by the conflict.[41] The lack of electricity and fuel for generators made pumping intermittent at best, and the potential for untreated wastewater to cross with drinking water was high.[42] The conditions for the spread of cholera were entirely predictable. And predicted. A UNICEF employee stated in 2018 that 'we are just one airstrike away from an unstoppable epidemic.'[43] Millions of cases followed. The epidemics came with the proliferation of the socioeconomic and biophysical ecosystems of the biosphere of war. And the consequences are likely to go well beyond the transmission of disease in Yemen if the situation in Gaza is at all comparable.

It is difficult today to imagine that Gaza's shallow water wells were once so sweet that every army invading or retreating from Egypt wanted to claim the territory. As the first or last place for their soldiers and war horses to refresh, the Babylonians, Romans, Ottomans, and British all sacrificed teenage soldiers to take the strip at the edge of the Sinai Desert.[44] Today, practically every drop of tap water in Gaza is too contaminated to drink, to the point that even the soap made with it is contaminated.[45] More than 90 per cent of the drinking water supplied by the municipality exceeds WHO drinking water guidelines for nitrates and 79 per cent for chlorides.[46] Roughly 40 per cent of water sampled at taps from two hospitals was found to be biologically contaminated in 2020—once again predictable and predicted, whenever the risk of

---

[39] See REACH.org, 'Secondary desk review on WASH assessments in Yemen (May 2020)' and Dureab et al., 'Cholera epidemic in Yemen.'
[40] UNICEF, Water Under Fire Volume 3.
[41] Indirect impacts of the longer-term aspects of the war were felt on the water providers' governance systems, bill collection rates, and staff (GIZ, 'Yemen water sector')—the latter in part because of the lack of salaries paid and also because of brain-drain (World Bank, 'Dynamic needs assessment').
[42] Al-Saidi, Roach, and Al-Saeedi, 'Conflict resilience of water and energy supply infrastructure: Insights from Yemen.'
[43] UNICEF, 'Yemen: Attacks on water facilities, civilian infrastructure, breach "basic laws of war."'
[44] Butt, Life at the Crossroads: A History of Gaza.
[45] Salama, 'Microbiological quality of soaps and efficacy of antiseptics and disinfectants used in hospitals in Gaza-Palestine,' and Altaher, 'Comparative identification of bacterial quality in liquid soap between Nasser and European Gaza hospitals, Khanyounis Governorate.'
[46] Palestinian Water Authority, 'Water resources status report.'

cross-contamination is considered.[47] Only about a quarter of the sewage is routinely treated, and it regularly seeps into the sea or into Gaza's main source of drinking water: the aquifer located just below the sand surface.[48]

Just about every toilet flushed or antibiotic secreted returns to the source (or to the sea) in a degraded state. The sewage from a toilet in an infectious disease hospital seeps without any treatment through the sand into the aquifer. There it joins water laced with pesticides from farms, heavy metals from industry, and ocean salts. It is then pumped back up by municipal or private wells, combined with a small fraction of freshwater sold by Israel, and cycled back into people's taps. No surprise to see the clear association between the Israeli attacks in 2014 and spikes in the incidence of killer diarrhoea.[49]

But there is something even more insidious lurking in the biosphere of Gaza's water: *antimicrobial resistance*—'superbugs' that are resistant to antibiotics and threaten to turn conventional medicine back more than one hundred years to when infections could not be stopped. Doctors who have been calling attention to this 'antibiotics apocalypse' for several years warn that more than 700,000 deaths are due to drug-resistant infections every year.[50] They blame overprescription of antibiotics in people, overuse in livestock production, and 'environmental factors' like water pipes where the resistant genes can mutate.[51] The result is that wounds that were not a concern a decade ago are life-threatening today.

The sheer number of infections in Gaza thus contribute to the runaway train of antimicrobial resistance. More than 13,000 people, proportionally equivalent to about 200,000 Brits, were targeted by Israeli snipers perched at the border during the Great March of Return demonstrations in 2018 and 2019. Another 2,000 were injured by the attacks in May 2021. Under these conditions, doctors reach for whatever drugs they have. Sometimes these are nearly expired carbapenems, two tonnes of which was dumped in Gaza in 2018 by donors, or ineffective first- and second-generation antibiotics because the more effective third- and fourth-generation ones are not available.

The manslaughter continues when the family that cannot be kept out of the wards returns to care for their injured loved one and transmit the nasties back home again. The biosphere has its own cycle: less regular access to clean water means infections will spread faster, bugs will be stronger, more antibiotics will be prescribed—and the victims will be further weakened. The spread of antimicrobial resistance through water is not confined to Gaza; it is a symptom of all urban biospheres of war. Just

---

[47] Shomar, 'Anti-microbial resistant bacteria in health care facilities: Exploring links with WASH - final report (Gaza AMR Pilot Study)'
[48] UNEP, Environmental Assessment of the Gaza Strip Following the Escalation of Hostilities in December 2008–January 2009.
[49] United Nations Relief and Works Agency (UNRWA), Epidemiological Bulletin for Gaza Strip.
[50] Cassini et al., 'Attributable deaths and disability-adjusted life-years caused by infections with antibiotic-resistant bacteria in the EU and the European Economic Area in 2015: a population-level modelling analysis.'
[51] Lamba, Graham, and Ahammad, 'Hospital wastewater releases of carbapenem-resistance pathogens and genes in urban India.'

ask the parents of the eight-year-old girl from Aleppo who arrived at the American University of Beirut in February 2020 with bilateral above-knee amputations and burns—and who died despite the tetracycline and colistin provided to her.[52] In this disastrous biosphere, patients are exposed in equal measure to viruses, superbugs, cephalosporins, and explosive missiles aimed at the hospitals where they are meant to be treated. Hospitals become Petri dish experiments; carers become carriers. 'Clean' water infects, soap kills.

The Rules of War

If we feel some sort of commitment to keep water out of the line of fire, we must confront the dark forces that drive war in the first place. Water crews all over the world do this again and again when they lay out the reasons to leave the water transmission infrastructure intact to the soldiers who rip up the ring road of the city they are besieging. Interrupting the water supply on top of imposing a curfew and stifling the city in other ways will only turn the otherwise unaligned people against them. Though appeals to win the 'hearts and minds' of the people they assault are rarely successful, many combatants do follow a code, especially when elders risk their lives to dialogue with them.

It may be impossible to tally the amount of misery that the courage of these human angels has prevented. It may also be too much to ask to replicate it. Apart from basic decency spread throughout society, the code would have to translate into legislation to grant all human beings not just equal rights and dignity, but also comparable safety from bombs. The former is not something that can be counted on; very often the fabric of society tears apart, and many people are soon hoarding water for their own families at the expense of others. The latter (the law) exists, too—but the rules are constantly eroded by inhumane and dehumanising actions on the battlefield and all who allow us to slip in that direction.

Policy and law will never carry the same moral weight and persuasion of the unwritten code. But it may give sufficient pause for thought to the commanding officers to restrain their soldiers somewhat. Building on efforts to criminalise 'ecocide,' initiatives like the Conflict and Environment Observatory and the Geneva Water Hub provide both the analyses and recommendations that political and military leaders require in order to protect the environment or water sources.[53] Furthermore, the UN Security Council issued Resolution 2573 in 2021, with the aim to protect essential services, like water and wastewater, during times of war.[54] These all build on the

---

[52] Personal communication with Dr Ghassan Abu Sitta, December 2017.
[53] Tignino and Irmakkesen, 'The Geneva list of principles on the protection of water infrastructure: An assessment and the way forward.'
[54] See UN Security Council Resolution 2573.

principles enshrined in the Rules of War, otherwise known as the Laws of Armed Conflict, the Geneva Conventions, or International Humanitarian Law.

Codified as International Humanitarian Law, the rules stipulate that a combatant can kill other combatants, but not civilians. They allow combatants to shoot each other with regular bullets, but not bullets whose full metal jacket has been filed off (because these explode on impact and cause more suffering than death). They stipulate that combatants are allowed to take and interrogate prisoners, but they must also provide them with water, shelter, food, and medical attention. You can rough them up, but you cannot gouge their eyes out with a spoon (or employ most other forms of torture). International Humanitarian Law exists to guide war, not to prevent or stop it. To make the hell more comfortable, the slaughter more civilised.

Nearing one thousand pages of conventions and protocols, International Humanitarian Law is a clunky instrument. It states that children cannot be targeted, not that they cannot be killed. In fact, children can be killed, legitimately, so long as the deaths are 'incidental' (i.e., collateral damage) and the combatants have followed the targeting rules of precaution and proportionality in attack. These rules state that the harm is proportionate to the military gain that may be achieved by the attack and that sufficient precaution has been taken to minimise the risk. The rule is a pragmatic admission that wars are (still) never fought only with precision weaponry. The proportionality assessment that must be carried out before the attack by targetters who follow International Humanitarian Law is meant to estimate the damage that might be done to civilians or the infrastructure that civilians rely on for survival. If the damage is deemed 'reasonably foreseeable,' precautions should be taken to avoid it, or the attack should not take place.[55] Therefore, some of the toddlers playing in the street near an arms depot become legitimate casualties. If they are even aware of the damage at all, the targetters may wring their hands, but they are protected with the full weight of the law against any recrimination. Legitimising atrocities is one reason Eyal Weizman refers to International Humanitarian Law as '665,' or one unit away from the number of the beast, in his book *The Least of All Possible Evils*.[56]

The norms that have been created about misuse or maltreatment of water during war are not as visceral as they are for children, even if the misery that results from them may be more traumatic than instant death (e.g., a messy death from cholera or wounds that never heal). International Humanitarian Law affords water workers no more theoretical protection than regular civilians. As they duct tape pipes together

---

[55] Robinson and Nohle, 'Proportionality and precautions in attack: the reverberating effects of using explosive weapons in populated areas,' and Nohle and Robinson, 'War in cities: The "reverberating effects" of explosive weapons.'

[56] Weizman, The Least of All Possible Evils, 6. The title of the book comes from Hannah Arendt's account of the complicity of the victims of Nazi horrors with the systems and people inflicting it when routinely faced with compliance or defiance with orders given. If they can assess that the moderation of violence is part of the very logic of violence, people who choose the 'lesser evil' in less extreme situations are still choosing evil and might do better to disrupt the system.

while dodging bullets, water workers are even more exposed to the risk of incidental damage than are most toddlers. But the letter of the law does not recognise this.

In the current world order, where the 1990s dreams of openness and adherence to international norms have been bad-mouthed from the highest of pulpits, we are forced to question the relevance of international law. Foreign policy is more inward-looking without being introspective, boisterously nationalistic. The workload of Human Rights Watch and Amnesty International keeps rising as they document violations of International Humanitarian Law and human rights at every turn. Preventing the harm in the first place would require statesmen to be held accountable for their actions so that their successors think twice. But the only warlords ever brought before the International Criminal Court are those who the international community has already abandoned—and who are no longer a threat to those who still profit from the established order. International law has very limited ability to deter, in the cynical view.

Yet the code that develops on one battlefield shapes the conduct of hostilities on other battlefields. Most combatants know that when one side raises the white flag, for example, they are calling for a cease fire, or at least negotiations. There is no morality here, just a very effective recognition that tit will lead to tat. If one side respects the white flag rule, it is so that the other side will do the same were the situation to be reversed. The same applies to mustard gas or blinding laser weapons—both simple enough technologies that were deployed during the Great Wars and caused horrifying injuries.

Traumatising and maiming a combatant through these means is a much more effective way of reaching military goals than killing because the rest of society is obligated to take care of the combatant for several decades. The cost of a substantial portion of a generation of young people who are so wounded is a heavy load for any society to bear. Seeing thousands of blind young men return to a community is more likely to end the support of that community for their government's war even faster than body bags would. Not long after World War II, most states signed up to the Rules of War, which stipulated that blinding weapons were not to be used, amongst an enormous volume of other rules.

International Humanitarian Law was not written with the intense interconnectedness of urban services in mind, so it is also completely blind to the indirect and cumulative impact of armed conflict and its reverberations on other services. In other words, International Humanitarian Law has no way to address the fact that the water pipes are effectively the lifelines of hospitals or that the electrical systems that power arms depots are essential to water treatment plants. This is a gaping hole in the shield that International Humanitarian Law is meant to be, one that requires urgent repair. The recent UNSC Resolution 2573 is one such patch. And there are opportunities for all who know about water systems to make International Humanitarian Law more effective. Perhaps even a duty.

Everyone who has lived through an extended conflict or who works regularly in war zones knows that there is a serious public health risk when a water or wastewater system goes down. Often enough, the risk becomes real, and disease and misery rip through society. The evidence base obliged to determine what effects are 'reasonably foreseeable' remains patchy. We have documented the effects of attacks on water systems quite well, and we have known the links between safe water and health for more than a century. We know less about the causality pathways, however, or the ways that an attack reverberates through the damaged water system onto human health, but the evidence base is growing. There is already enough experience and data to argue that it would not be unreasonable to expect an outbreak of infectious disease if a wastewater treatment plant was damaged and if its proximity to drinking water sources or infrastructure meant there was a high risk of cross-contamination between water and wastewater lines, for example.[57]

This poses a challenge to military lawyers. Sometimes they express resentment about the creep of International Humanitarian Law's jurisdiction into the very complex environments that are biospheres of war. If it becomes reasonable to foresee that incidental damage to a water or wastewater treatment plant might contribute to the spread of cholera, after all, this will oblige the military's targetters to weigh the thousands of deaths expected against the tactical gain of the attack. The more that we can catalogue the direct, indirect, and cumulative impact of attacks on water services, the less anybody can claim ignorance. This might lead, possibly, somewhere, someday, to a reduction in the spread of disease and amount of suffering. Military lawyers who argue against this mounting body of knowledge may be even more distant from the harm they cause indirectly than the snipers who wait by a water source to pull the trigger on the people found in their crosshairs.

---

[57] Talhami and Zeitoun, 'The impact of attacks on urban services II: Reverberating effects of damage to water and wastewater systems on infectious disease.'

4
Hostile Waters

> Every empire, however, tells itself and the world that it is unlike all other empires, that its mission is not to plunder and control but to educate and liberate.
>
> —Edward Said, *The Blind Arrogance of the Imperial Gaze*

Water molecules trying to stick together and ejecting the ice cube that was dropped into them.

Source: Author.

If we are so willing to run the rivers red, snipe thirsty mothers, deny water to some while providing it to others, turn off the taps to neighbourhoods full of children, and ignore evidence and laws which link damage to water systems with disease, what is to stop our states and national representatives from warring over water? Nothing, really. And yet there has never been a 'water war.' The environmental peace-making community reiterate this point at every turn. Apart from the war between the kingdoms of Lagash and Umma more than two and a half millennia ago, they point out, no two states have ever gone to war primarily over water.[1]

---

[1] TFDD, 'Transboundary Freshwater Dispute Database.'

Perhaps this is the expression of our informed water ethos of care? Unfortunately, the assertion is technically accurate but way off target. In fact, interstate struggles over international watercourses play out very differently to the killing and maiming of the previous chapter. International water conflicts are all about state hoarding: either exerting the most control they can over transboundary flows or maximising the use or degrading the quality of the water itself. Greed is buttressed by nationalism and violent expressions of asymmetries in power.

The hoarding can be so extreme and entrenched that the suffering from international water conflicts can be just as terrible as war. Livelihoods are ruined by human-caused drought, families are ripped apart when children are forced to migrate, injustices are perpetuated and remembered for centuries. It does not matter at all that there are no 'water wars' per se: international water conflicts abound and cause all manner of misery.

The key actor in international water conflicts is the state apparatus of the more powerful nation, which has control over the transboundary flows. Can you think of a situation where the arrangement over transboundary flows does not favour the more powerful state? In dry areas, this means the regional or river basin hegemon gets more water. In wet areas, the basin hegemon has the choice to store the water upstream or release it downstream. In all cases, it is the prerogative of the more powerful actor to consolidate control of the waters or share them. When the hegemon chooses to hoard, it is the marginalised communities in the less powerful states that suffer the most, like the woman making *labneh* in the West Bank who is prevented by Israeli soldiers from capturing the rain.

International water conflicts are thus part and parcel of the militarised political economic structures that have led to the folly and destruction seen in earlier chapters. The politics, economics, armed conflict, and political conflict manage to creep into each other's stories. There are also a few twists that makes international water conflicts fascinating to study: most are related to hydraulic missions which are conducted under the current political economy (dams, in many cases) and almost all contain an element of international 'cooperation' that is not always welcome and sometimes deceitful. Such is the case not least of all on the Nile, Jordan, and Tigris and Euphrates Rivers, which we will explore in greater detail here. First, we must reflect on how we get water wars and water peace so wrong, concluding with a discussion on international water law and the politics that have not yet managed to displace it as the least-worst guide of water diplomacy.

Why we don't wage war over water

Hoarding and structural violence cannot be photographed. International water conflicts will not be televised. Having said this, international water conflicts do attract more media attention than greening deserts, the fracturing of society when the taps are turned off, or old women denied the rain. This may be partly because of our general fascination with geopolitics and a penchant to be armchair generals and rulers. Water evokes a particular strain of passion and nationalism, especially when stripped of its complexity and presented simplistically.

Whatever the reason, books sell and websites bait better when they scream 'Water Wars!' Think tanks produce global heatmaps to draw attention to ongoing tensions or predict future conflict. Inevitably, they present entire regions, and sometimes entire countries, in a single colour as if they were homogenous. As eye-catching as the graphics are, the analysis does not really stand up. After all, the water problems in monsoonal southern India are nothing like those in the desert north-west of the same country. And the effects of water conflicts that are felt in Nepal and Bangladesh are very different from each other, and totally distinct from those felt in India—even though all are in the Ganges Basin. In any case, there is nothing uniform about international transboundary water conflicts. Their entire character can change radically in just a few years and, at any time, are experienced entirely differently for downstreamers, midstreamers, and upstreamers.

Much of the analysis you read about concerning international water conflicts links them with biophysical water scarcity and the message that water scarcity leads to conflict (or climate change leads to water scarcity leads to conflict). The social element of scarcity is far too often greatly underconsidered. That is to say, too much analysis suggests that the amount of water available is something people have not already adapted to and will therefore fight over it. At the same time, these analyses ignore the unfair distribution of water, as if this does not contribute to tension.

There is perhaps no other dimension of water that the misunderstings of Chapter 1 have created so many problems. It might be different if water was worth much in our economies. Recall that the great bulk of water 'used' by humans—that is, the water that is put beyond our immediate control and back into the biosphere—is to grow food. Selling Andean asparagus to Europe is lucrative indeed, but half a billion dollars annually will not get any state very far, especially considering how much effort it takes to produce it. A sizeable aquifer or river can grow a thousand tonnes of carrots and cabbage, but it is a long and tortuous path from cash crops to cash.

It is easier to exploit diamonds or oil. Such 'conflict resources' can sustain a costly war effort and self-justify the risks taken during wars. The United States and United Kingdom did not invade Iraq to control its date production. Matching the net worth of the annual production for an average Iraqi oil field would take more than three hundred annual harvests of Iraqi dates (assuming these were as valuable as Peruvian asparagus).[2] Perhaps water would be worth starting a war for if it was easier to steal. But each litre of water weighs one kilogramme. Meaning each cubic metre—the amount you drink in a year—weighs one metric tonne, and the steak you ate at lunch virtually weighs four and a half tonnes. It takes a lot of energy to move water around: about ten

---

[2] At US$100 per barrel and 2017 production rates—see YCharts, 'Iraq Crude Oil Production', ycharts.com/indicators/iraq_crude_oil_production.

joules to lift one cubic metre one metre high. The cost of transporting water—if an army were ever to attempt it—could cost much more than it's worth.

On the other hand, water certainly does have symbolic value—another reason why men have proven extremely willing to kill others for it. Water is central to many religious rituals for cleansing, healing, and rebirth.[3] Millions of Christian pilgrims visit Christ's baptism site on the Jordan River, and the confluence of the tributaries to the Ganges are considered holy sites in Buddhist and Hindu practices. But under what conditions might the symbolic or metaphysical value of water ever outweigh its limited economic value and difficulty to move it, to the point that it is the main reason for a war? Not many. Recall Tony Allan's observation that food imports and virtual water take the edge off tense international relations.[4] States that do not have enough water to grow all their own food often rely on the water available in other countries and then import the latter's food. The tensions on the Nile might have resulted in violence if the government of Egypt could not import any food. But it can. And it does—to the equivalent of roughly one-third of the flow of the Nile every year.[5] Importing food is a great way to hide water mismanagement, and it helps when deciding whether it's worth fighting a war.

Why we don't wage peace over water

Ground-breaking description of databases of water events has backed the point of the lack of water wars empirically and emphasises the volume of observable 'cooperation' over water sources.[6] In countering the journalistic 'water scarcity leads to war' narrative, some policymakers draw a similarly simple message: water can lead to cooperation and maybe even peace. But there are at least two reasons to dig deeper if we want to support diplomacy that leads to less suffering from water conflicts: assumptions of causal direction and misunderstanding the term 'cooperation.' Each is influenced by power plays that are ever-present when one side has a preponderance of power. When one considers the effects of power asymmetry alongside a state's position on a river, one gets a clear indication of the politics that are not verbalised—and inroads to the voices that are less heard.

Confusing correlation with causation

A thorny issue arises from the classic mistake of mixing statistical correlation and causation when trawling the databases. As the sophisticated algorithms of the

---

[3] See Wolf, *The Spirit of Dialogue* and Marks, *The Holy Order of Water*.
[4] See Allan, *Virtual Water*.
[5] Zeitoun, Allan, and Mohieldeen, 'Virtual water "flows" of the Nile Basin, 1998–2004: A first approximation and implications for water security.'
[6] See TFDD and Wolf, 'Shared waters.'

satirical website Spurious Correlations points out, there is a statistically significant relation between the number of people who died in a swimming pool in the United States every year from 1999 to 2009 and the number of films that Nicolas Cage appeared in during that same decade.[7] However, significant correlation does not mean that one parameter caused the other. While the pool deaths–Nicolas Cage example shows the absurdity of assuming causality, many think-tanks fall into this trap when they seek to communicate messages from the water events databases. The fact that there are more events deemed 'cooperative' in the database than 'conflictive' leads some to the conclusion that 'water is a catalyst for peace.' Some publications designed to support water diplomats even assert that 'Any two countries engaged in active water cooperation do not go to war for any other reason,' a bold claim with dubious backing.[8]

Despite the misrepresentation of data, these is a sincere appreciation for the life-providing and irreplaceable essence of water throughout such efforts. 'We value water too much to hoard it for ourselves,' goes the narrative.[9] These thinkers tend to be overtly or covertly positivist in disciplines as wide as politics, international relations, archaeology, anthropology, and environmental science. But whether this perspective is 'reality' or confirmation bias, the pendulum has swung too far back in some policy circles. To suggest that there is something inherent in water that compels states to cooperate is a harmful oversimplification because it means that the destructive side of water conflicts is downplayed, wished away, or ignored.

The problem with both the 'water leads to war' and 'water leads to peace' narratives is that they reflect environmentally deterministic thinking. That is, they assume that the environment determines interstate relations, whereas in the reality that I experience, it is the relations between states that determine how they interact over the environment. Like many others, I wish that healthy and beautiful biospheres inspired and shaped international relations. But what I have seen tells me that water does not drive but is subordinate to decision-making in politics. In any case, there is no empirical basis to think that water scarcity or abundance will lead to peace, and the assertion's logic rests on fallacious assumptions.[10]

---

[7] 'Number people who drowned by falling into a swimming-pool correlates with number of films Nicolas Cage appeared in,' Spurious Correlations.

[8] The assertion may come from the 'Golden Arches Theory of Conflict Prevention,' which is the name given by its detractors to Thomas Friedman's 1996 assertion that 'No two countries that both have a McDonald's have ever fought a war against each other,' and which has been ably discredited—see Musgrave, 'The Beautiful, Dumb Dream of McDonald's Peace Theory.'

[9] For instance Wolf et al. assert that water is so important that nations cannot afford to fight over it in 'Navigating peace: Water can be a pathway to peace, not war.'

[10] Selby, Daoust, and Hoffmann, in *Divided Environments*, call this 'eco-determinism' and call it the unthinking 'Zombie theory of politics.' See also Forsyth, *Critical Political Ecology*.

Lazy thinking about 'cooperation'

We will need less deterministic and much more pragmatic analysis if we want to ease the suffering that water conflicts cause. International tension over water is often (though not always) part of a bigger picture of interstate relations that include historical enmity, revenge, the personal ambitions of leaders, economics, geopolitics, identity, injustices—to name just a few. Political ecology theory nestled within international political economy theory suggests that the most that can be said with any certainty is that water may in part reduce or may in part increase international tensions. Although this framework generates fewer headlines, when applied to particular cases, the theory is very helpful. Case studies may be less attractive than heatmaps but remain the best method upon which to found diplomacy.

There are loads of examples of states sorting out their water issues and sometimes quite creatively. The coordination between France and Switzerland over Lake Geneva led to a mutually agreed redrawing of the border. Similarly, we can draw hope from the fact that the United States and Canada had the prescience in the 1940s to insert a fifty-year revising clause in their agreement over the Columbia River. The nations renegotiated this very constructively and on time, and they resolved it in just the past few years.

Most people live in tougher neighbourhoods, however. It would be imprudent to draw too many lessons learned from present-day Central Europe or northern North America. Along the headwaters of the Indus River in Kashmir, people are dying and killing just to establish the Indian–Pakistani border itself. Jordanians and Palestinians are locked into the most inflexible of water treaties. Egyptian leaders have threatened to bomb the Ethiopian capital or coerce the Sudanese capital over upstream dams. Iranian and Turkish soldiers are engaged in proxy battles along the Tigris and Euphrates, and both states have ongoing conflict against political and military movements of Kurdish people who reside in the headwaters. Any temptation to apply lessons about cooperation from states that have nourished decades of peaceful relations to these well-known hotspots must be resisted.

In any case, what does 'cooperation' even mean? It could just mean coordination, or it could mean dialogue. Does it necessarily mean co-management and the sharing of power over decisions? It is helpful to be clear what we mean when we use the term because so many have experienced it as something sinister. Negative interpretations of cooperation fall in the vein of collaborating with the enemy, a means to suppress critical voice or thought, or unquestioning obedience to the established order. Just like the torturer whose threats force his prisoner to 'cooperate' by divulging the information or confession sought, the privilege to define the meaning of terms lies with those who have more power. The weaker party usually ends up 'cooperating' on the stronger party's terms, whether out of fear, ingrained subordination, or strategically—to better alter their current or future position in the relationship.

The great bulk of research on international water conflicts is equally loose with the definition of water cooperation. Just as the World Bank urged Ethiopian officials to 'cooperate' with Egypt in the early days of the Nile Basin Initiative, or as US intermediaries pressed Palestinians to 'cooperate' with Israelis during the Oslo II process, the international community often suggests to representatives of Iraq and Afghanistan that they 'cooperate' over transboundary waters with Iran. When the less-powerful parties eventually accede to the encouragement, the action is lazily misinterpreted by analysts as working towards the same goal.

Such digging never gets very far past the surface and may also rely on an unchecked assumption that cooperation and peace are two sides of the same coin, and that both are the opposite of conflict and war. Yet, as we saw in Chapter 3, peace often looks like war, particularly when the civilians of the losing side bear the brunt of conditions resulting from the victory or temporary end of outright hostilities.

Similarly, conflict and cooperation coexist. Anyone who lives with another person knows that. You can be bickering with each other as you go to collect groceries (fighting and gathering at the same time). The fact is reflected in hundreds of poems about the human condition, as well as in thought.[11] Lauded professor of philosophy and economics Amartya Sen used the term 'cooperative conflicts' to describe the way that some subjected individuals or groups engage with the processes presented to them as a means towards the ends they desire.[12] While social liberals would allow the creation of more space for alternative voices and the agency of others than their conservative counterparts would, the boundaries of any asymmetric relationship remain fixed, and the degree of freedom granted could never be more than what is required to maintain the order.

It is the same for interstate interaction over transboundary waters. Environmental politics expert Naho Mirumachi even invented an elegant tool to allow analysis of co-existing conflict and cooperation over transboundary waters.[13] The dynamics and nuance of the water conflict can be better characterised when relations between two states are plotted along the tool's intensifying degrees of 'conflict,' defined in terms of security studies theory, and 'cooperation,' defined in terms of psychological theory. Application of this strategy in dozens of contexts has led researchers to distinguish between legal and outcome-oriented cooperation[14] and to be more understanding of constructive forms of conflict and wary of destructive forms of cooperation.[15] Water diplomats should know when a party has been dragged to the table and informed of the options, as opposed to coming willingly to a discussion, if they seek to resolve rather than conceal grievances.

---

[11] As W. H. Auden noted: 'If equal affection cannot be, let the more loving one be me.'
[12] See Sen, 'Gender and cooperative conflicts,' in *Persistent Inequalities*.
[13] See Mirumachi, *Transboundary Water Politics in the Developing World*.
[14] See McCraken, *Defining Effective Transboundary Water Cooperation*.
[15] See Zeitoun, Mirumachi, and Warner, *Water Conflicts*.

Why we do fight over water

In between water wars and water peace is the real-world tension and suffering of water conflicts. Most of the stress is due to the jarring dissonance between the fluidity of water, a fact of nature, and static political borders, a human construct.[16] Rivers flow across borders set in rivers; aquifers pass underneath these borders; clouds above them. Likewise, forests, savannas, and oceans spread across the surface of the Earth without a mind to the geopolitical boundaries created by humans. We could scarcely have more poorly designed our international political system to live within our natural habitat. This is doubly the case when you consider that states industrialise at different rates and the extreme prejudice that nationalism encourages.

Rivers compel states to do what many would rather avoid: interact with each other. Border dams reveal this most clearly. Upstream on five rivers in a very tough neighbourhood, some forty Afghan guards were killed before the government inaugurated the Kamal Khan dam on the border of Iran in March 2021. One month later, six civilians were killed when upstream Kyrgyz and downstream Tajik security forces clashed over a land dispute sparked by the filling of a Soviet-era reservoir.

Downstream states usually get the jump on upstream states. Human settlement has always centred around the cultivation of the flatter and more fertile areas at the end of rivers and all the river sediment deposited there. In the case of the Nile, the downstream development may be occuring thousands of years after so many different cultures had perfected irrigation techniques in lower Egypt but is still a full century before the recent upstream Ethiopian efforts to harness the river. Likewise, ongoing Turkish hydropower dams and Iranian diversion schemes on the Tigris or Euphrates rivers follow Iraqi national development projects which were completed four or five decades earlier. Israel drained the Huleh marshes, dammed the Lake of Tiberias, and undertook extensive groundwater development from the 1950s to the 1970s at least half a century before the governments of upstream Lebanon and side stream Palestinian Authority started on the dams and deep wells that still seek to build on a tributary of the Jordan River and transboundary aquifers.

The hydraulic missions of downstream states provided them a measure of control over their communities and helped them flourish economically. But the downstream state structures also became dependent on the levels of water use that they had established. This leaves the downstreamers vulnerable to any upstream water development projects. It is a recipe for disaster in an age where so many upstream states are charging on with their own hydraulic missions. Crucially, and to the possible detriment of the downstreamers, the upstreamers maintain sovereignty over the territory where the transboundary flows originate. Dams and

---

[16] Having said this, the boundary-pushing work of Kimberley Thomas on water conflicts and borders presents a much more subtle and interesting way to conceive the border–basin dissonance; see, e.g., Thomas, 'The river-border complex' and 'The Ganges water treaty'.

desert-blooming projects on the drawing board or under construction in Ethiopia, Lebanon, Turkey, and Iran thus generate impacts that downstreamers now have to contend with.

However, a state's location on a river or watercourse does not determine the outcome of any water conflict. If the upstream state is also the more powerful, it may dictate the terms of its intentions, as Turkey did on the Euphrates. If the upstream state is less powerful than its downstream neighbours, it must negotiate the terms of its intentions.[17] Only very skilful diplomacy that harnesses fortuitous timing and international standards could transform the tensions in this context, but third parties cast for the role typically undertake weathervane diplomacy and seek to avoid or at best manage tensions rather than deal with them.

Hoarding on the Tigris and Euphrates

Such is the case on the Tigris and Euphrates, where the impact of the flows diverted in upstream Turkey and Iran is felt first and foremost by the farmers at the tail end of the rivers, in Iraq. All of which is happening in a vacuum of international media attention and diplomacy.

For hundreds of thousands of years, both the Euphrates and the Tigris Rivers have been eroding the hard rock mountains of south-eastern Anatolia as they flow southwards towards the Persian Gulf. The Tigris has also been gorged by healthy tributaries flowing in from the east. The flood pulses of both rivers collide during the (Northern Hemisphere's) winter and spring months, in the desert at al-Qurnah with its hot sun, loads of water, and vast quantities of extremely fertile silt. With plenty of blossoms and abundant and sleek livestock, it is the original land of milk and honey. Beneath the rivers at this point lies a bed of clay so thick and pure that it supported all the pottery and art that the local entrepreneurs could fashion with it. Through their ingenuity and effort, these conditions were managed so that food was abundant and civilisation flourished.

This is ancient Mesopotamia or *Bain al nahrein*, meaning the 'land between the rivers.' The land so coveted and contested by Ur and Uruk, the Akkadians, Babylonians, Cyrus the Great, Darius the Great, Alexander the Great, Saddam Hussein, and George Bush, Jr. These are the Rivers of Babylon, on whose banks the Jewish slaves captured by King Nebuchadnezzar wept for their return to Zion. This is where the patriarch Abraham lived, where Hammurabi wrote the first law many centuries earlier. Go back further still, and humankind itself is credited with originating from this land. This is the Garden of Eden, where the creation myth holds humans failed their first test to resist the urge to acquire. Fast forward to the turn of the twenty-first century CE, and there was a scraggly apple tree that local entrepreneurs claimed belonged to Adam,

---

[17] See Allan, *The Middle East Water Question*.

Figure 4.1 Water intake structure for a village on the Euphrates River near its confluence with the Tigris River just before it was extended for the second time in Iraq, 2001.
Source: Author.

'the first man.' Parked next to it was a small white van emblazoned with 'Adam's Ice Cream' in Arabic and English.

Precious little silt makes it to the meeting point today. It gets stuck behind the series of dams that have been built upstream. First, the Haditha Dam in Iraq, then the Tabqa Dam in Syria, and the Atatürk Dam in Turkey. Each were built and presented as symbols of national pride. On the Tigris, Turkey has recently completed the Ilisu Dam, displacing the people of the ancient Akkadian and modern Kurdish village of Hasankeyf, and altering the flow downstream. Taken together, the villages, archaeological sites, and ecosystems that these dams submerged were not really matched by the benefits that were promised, and they are all good examples of bad dams (to return to Chapter 2).[18]

As a result, the once-rich confluence is poor, and the crescent is no longer fertile; paradise has been lost. In the early 1950s, the managers of the village water treatment plants which had been built on the banks of the tail end of the Euphrates were forced to extend their intake structures several dozen metres out into the river, where it was just deep enough to draw up the water. They had to be extended a second time by the turn of the century because the waters kept receding, as water was held back upstream (Figure 4.1). It is an easy enough task, with heavy construction equipment, to dig up the clay of the riverbed, which remains so pure that it takes very little effort to fashion

---

[18] Anyone interested in dams and who also appreciates the art of storytelling is encouraged to see Omar Amiraley's documentary on the topic: 'Flood in Ba'ath Country', https://www.imdb.com/title/tt0455950/. The film is a retrospective of the benefits of the dam decades after its construction and makes great use of the footage the filmmaker made at the time of its construction, when he was a graduate fresh out of university and more hopeful for the benefits.

an ashtray or cup from. Twenty years on, and with upstream hydraulic missions in full swing, the intake structures are reaching out further for a third time.

The upstream infrastructure has caused the rivers to flow so slowly that the tide from the Persian Gulf carries seawater hundreds of kilometres up the Shatt al-Arab river to poison the water and kill the soil at the confluence. Salinity levels of the Euphrates at al-Qurnah are in the vicinity of several thousand parts per million. So salty that no suds form in the soap when you shower. So salty that when Basra's water was no longer fit to drink in the 1980s, the Iraqi government had to source its new scheme several hundreds of kilometres upriver, where the water was still fresh. This canal shows the devastation of the attacks during the 2003 US–UK invasion of Iraq, where the impact of the sanctions before it and the violence after the invasion accumulated to the point that the residents of Basra were dying from cholera in 2015, or being beaten while protesting about it in 2018 (as discussed in Chapter 3). The hourglass-shaped palm trees in the suburban Basra gardens reflect the quality of the water very clearly. Trees planted in the 1970s started to widen out with improved water in and around the 1980s, but have since narrowed again from 2003 onwards.[19]

Things are very different thousands of kilometres upstream. The Atatürk Dam on the Euphrates has proven so successful at holding back the headwaters that the original irrigation schemes have been extended in every direction. Following the 'crops per drop' and 'dollars per drop' logic of irrigation efficiency (Chapter 2), new orchards of almond and pistachio trees are planted right up to the very edge of the border of Syria. The plantations are huge: 'California-sized' is the comparison drawn by guides to help tourists get their heads around it.[20] Indeed, gazing through binoculars to try to gauge the extent of the project, what becomes perfectly clear is that the western United States, home to iconic water problems, has not only inspired the enterprise, but put it into direct competition in the global nut trade. Inspired by the Tennessee Valley, the new Atatürk fields may soon reach the schemes resulting from the Ilisu Dam filled by the Tigris hundreds of kilometres to the east. Fruit and vegetables abound, thousands of jobs have been created, and resistance to the loss of Kurdish culture and biodiversity inside Turkey has been temporarily quashed.

Iran also is diverting the westward flowing tributaries to the Tigris back in on themselves. Deep into their the late-period hydraulic mission, water 'resource' managers are tasked to refill Lake Urmia and ensure the Zayandeh Rud river flows through the (once-Safavid capital of) Isfahan continuously again. Already under pressure from Iraqi dams, the Diyala River flowing to meet the Tigris just upstream of Baghdad dries out as a result. The tributaries diverted in Iran's southern Khuzestan province affect the local (mainly Arab) population just as much, leading to Detroit- and Basra-style water protests in 2021.

Still recovering from the US–UK invasion of 2003, the Iraqi state is in a poor position to defend its national priorities and interests, such as the hydrological impact on

---

[19] Personal communication with water engineer in southern Iraq, 1998, 2006.
[20] Personal communication with guide, 2012.

its own dams,[21] let alone the wellbeing of its farmers. So the Iraqi farmers are left with few good options. They end up buying food grown with the water from farms in the upstream states, instead of growing it themselves. This looks like a virtual water 'solution' as people make do with less water, guided by the 'invisible hand' of the forces which drive political markets. The farmers see it differently than European analysts, however. For them, this is a humiliation and a great source of resentment. The tension will have to rise to the surface at some point. Groups like Save the Tigris and other nongovernmental organisations (NGOs) try valiantly to resist, but, like the farmers, they are more spectators than players in this game. The best anyone can do is to send their sons and daughters off to the capitals to look for a way to earn a living.

These arrangements are not enshrined in treaties, but memoranda of understanding are restricting options. For instance, the 2019 Turkey–Iraq memorandum of understanding (MOU) facilitates upstream dam construction and encourages technical cooperation to improve downstream irrigation efficiency.[22] The downstream communities are told they should be using whatever water reaches them more effectively, rather than sorting out joint management of the river or an equitable sharing of the water. Instead of relieving the stress of social water scarcity, virtual water locks in a situation that should not (and cannot, really) be sustained.

Instead of transboundary water management, we have an uncoordinated series of dams. We have hoarding instead of sharing and dependence instead of creativity. Destructive cooperation instead of constructive cooperation. We are left with the result of a combination of nationalist hydraulic missions in a strongly structured political economy that is heavily shaped by decades of war and international sanctions. The 'need' for the upstream water was created recently and is not something that can be easily given up. Almond blossoms now flourish where culture once did, to flavour the coffees of Europe. Apart from turn-of-the-century efforts by the World Bank and UNESCO, we also have very little diplomacy and next to no international attention.

Hoarding on the Nile

Many farmers who draw on the Nile suffer a similar fate. The river has sustained farms for four thousand years at least and has been associated with the country of Egypt for nearly as long. The 'father of history' Herodotus himself is claimed to have said that 'Egypt is the Nile, and the Nile is Egypt.' It does not rain much at all anywhere in the country, and there are few other sources of water in the country apart from groundwater near the delta at the Mediterranean Sea. Egypt really *is* the Nile, especially for the millions of farmers who make up the base of the state's economy.

---

[21] Al-Madhhachi et al., 'Hydrological impact of Ilisu Dam on Mosul Dam; the River Tigris.'
[22] Dawood, 'Does the memorandum of understanding in water management between Turkey and Iraq guarantee Iraq its water rights?' in *Water Forum. Save the Tigris.*

But the Nile is not just Egypt. As the longest river in the world, the Nile flows from rain falling on parts of Eritrea, Tanzania, Kenya, Uganda, Rwanda, the Democratic Republic of Congo, Sudan, South Sudan, and—especially—Ethiopia. With its headwaters in the rain forest, the basin of the Nile borders on the basin of the Congo River. This means that if you are standing on the right mountain ridge in Uganda and spit towards the Nile, you are contributing to the world's longest river. If you turn your head, you are contributing to the world's second biggest river in terms of volume, following only the Amazon.

After turbulent starts at Lake Victoria and Lake Tana, the White and Blue Niles join at Khartoum/Omdurman in Sudan and snake tranquilly during the dry months for thousands of kilometres through the desert towards Egypt and the Mediterranean. The river gorges from January to May, spawned by heavy rainfall in Eastern and Central Africa. When it dissipates, the flood pulse deposits the precious silt on which the famers grow crops. The practice of planting on the receding land is called 'recession agriculture.'

This is the land of Ancient Egypt, whose rulers gave their people hieroglyphics and built pyramids. This is the Kingdom of Kush from which the Nubian civilisation emerged. Farmlands on the banks are made this fertile by the mountain minerals that the river erodes, and already good diets can be complemented by fish from the river and the yoghurt of the nomadic peoples wandering past the edge of the palms into the desert. Another land of milk and honey, where architecture and art combined in elegant and striking house paintings which have been described by historian Herman Bell as 'an outward expression of an inner grace.'[23] And during roughly the same period that Hammurabi was codifying social rules that were being established between the Tigris and Euphrates, the Meroitic empire came to dominate the Nile around the fourth cataract, building hundreds of more pyramids to honour its leaders.

With so much to gain from watering the fertile soil, irrigation techniques became very sophisticated, evolving from human-driven levers and Archimedes screws to camel-driven pumps (see Figure 2.3 and Box 2.1 'Dams on the Nile'). The same ingenuity was on display the minute that low-lift petrol and diesel pumps became available, prompting Sudanese novelist Tayeb Salih to reflect,

> From my position under the tree I saw the village slowly undergo a change: the waterwheels disappeared to be replaced on the bank of the Nile by pumps, each one doing the work of a hundred water-wheels. I saw the bank retreating year after year in front of the thrustings of the water, while on another part it was the water that retreated. Sometimes strange thoughts would come to my mind. Seeing the bank contracting at one place and expanding at another, I would think that such was life: with a hand it gives, with the other it takes.[24]

---

[23] Personal communication, 2017.
[24] Salih, *Season of Migration to the North*, 4.

Once Egyptian farmers had steadily planted right up to the new edge of the riverbed and were hooked into buying fertilisers, the government had no choice but to continue to hold back the flows, even in very wet years. President Mubarak seized the opportunity to create the Toshka Lakes, a California-sized agricultural scheme. Producing food in a place with the world's highest evapo-transpiration rates and no population is possibly also a world-beating case of Desert Bloom Syndrome. The vulnerability and potential of the scheme was revealed following several years of lower flows, but it has since taken on a renewed urgency in post-2011 revolution Egypt.

Before considering the implications of this revolution on the Nile conflict, let us return to the fourth cataract where the Sudanese government, under former President Omar al-Bashir, completed the Merowe Dam in 2008. All rulers of Egypt or Kush have gone to great lengths to reduce risks to the state or kingdom. This includes threatening Ethiopia with war (as recently as 2014) and collusion with the upstream governments of Sudan, hence the signature of the 1959 Nile Agreement between the two countries, from which Sudan's Merowe Dam emerged.

Even if the Merowe Dam may have been perceived to have threatened Egypt's national water security (as Ethiopia's Grand Ethiopian Renaissance Dam [GERD] does today), it was built entirely with Egyptian consent—in no small part because it blocked a lot of the sediment that was filling Lake Nasser and thus already reducing the amount of electricity that the Aswan High Dam could produce.[25] Judging by the fact that Sudanese farmers situated between the Merowe and the Aswan High dams must now buy fertilisers to continue farming, the Merowe Dam is in this way successful. As we saw in Chapter 2, the Merowe is by all other measures a bad dam—not least of all for the Amri, Hamdab, and Manasir people who were displaced by it (Figure 4.2).[26]

The same 1959 Nile Agreement is at the heart of international tensions in northeastern Africa. Although based on absolute volumetric terms, the agreement allocates roughly 85 per cent of the water to Egypt, 15 per cent to Sudan. This leaves none for Ethiopia or any of the other Nile states. That allocation is challenged head-on by Ethiopia's construction of the GERD. The geopolitical picture has changed considerably in the meantime, most significantly because of the political revolution in Egypt and the subsequent strengthening of the Ethiopian military. The GERD is sure to alter the flow and amount of sediment carried by the river to Sudan and Egypt in a big way. The Sudanese farmers downstream of the GERD will be forced to adapt, just as those who were impacted by the Merowe and Aswan Dams were forced to adapt. That is, they will buy phosphates and nitrogen to maintain their yields once the fertile silt is denied to them for the first time in history. Like the farmers in Iraq, they will send their children to work as labourers

---

[25] If there is more sediment in the reservoir, there is less of a head (or height) of water, which means the turbines will flow more slowly and less electricity will be created.
[26] Dirar, *Valuing Property in the Manasir Communities near the Merowe Dam*.

Figure 4.2 A farmer rowing a boat over a Manasir village submerged by the reservoir of the Merowe Dam on the fourth cataract of the Nile River, Sudan, 2018.
Photo by Azza Dirar

in the cities, to live as wage-slaves, because they cannot survive on the land. The adaptation is so silent that decision-makers are not usually forced to confront the consequences of their choices, conveniently enough.

While the driving forces and consequences of the Nile conflict are very similar to those of the Tigris and Euphrates, the Nile receives a different league of media attention and diplomacy. This started early on through the Canadian International Development Agency and World Bank-driven Nile Basin Initiative (NBI). The NBI allowed for a genuine effort at cooperation. Until the 2011 political revolution, Egypt was heavily involved in driving the NBI and promoted cooperation of just about any sort, at just about every turn. With the flexible state of hegemony that Egypt had established over the Nile flows, few analysts expected that the more powerful downstream state's overuse of the flows would ever change.[27] As such, the World Bank supported all initiatives put forward by other Nile countries, but only so long as they did not threaten the distribution established by the neo-colonial and bilateral 1959 Nile Agreement.

The donors supported the projects that Egypt supported, such as producing high-resolution vegetation indices, mapping evapo-transpiration rates, or establishing a Nile Basin Commission. They firmly opposed the Ethiopian (and sometimes Sudanese) requests to renegotiate or replace the 1959 Agreement even as they hailed the great 'cooperation' between the former enemies—and whose talk shops could be photographed and spread across the front pages of newspapers. As opposition to

---

[27] Ana Cascão excepted: see Cascão, 'Changing power relations in the Nile river basin' and 'GERD: new norms of cooperation in the Nile Basin?'

a process that built slowly over the decades, the narrative developed by the World Bank in response was consistently a form of 'Don't bring politics into this,' along with attempts to portray critics as anti-development.

The unfairly mediated process notwithstanding, the Ethiopian government remained engaged in the NBI throughout, 'cooperating' in a quite strategic manner and with longer-term goals in sight. As the power balance began to shift, and especially from around 2008 onwards, the World Bank found itself backing the wrong horse, and its staff were no longer welcome in Addis Ababa or Khartoum. One highly ranked influencer even became persona non grata for continuously promoting the Egyptian position and discounting the positions of others.[28]

The political dynamics changed substantially with Ethiopia's decision to follow through with the NBI's draft Framework Agreement at this time. The Framework Agreement ever-so-slightly suggested that the existing allocation of the flows should be reconsidered, and the cat was out of the bag. For several years and particularly after the revolution in Egypt, Ethiopia led the weakened downstream states in negotiations about the new river flow regime following their planned construction of the GERD. Reservoir-filling and dam-release strategies provided more accurate predictions of the severity of the impact downstream.

At some point during the process, a change in tune became discernible from many analysts and diplomats in Egypt as they began calling for international water law to guide upstream behaviour. The narrative changed, as well, in the sense that ongoing Egyptian claims of Ethiopian 'hydro-hegemony' replaced the old Ethiopian assertions that Egypt held sway over the mediators. As recently as late 2019, however, the US Treasury under the Trump administration reverted to the pre-revolution stance of the World Bank and began openly and blatantly pushing the preferred Egyptian position. Critics openly state that US mediation has amounted to little more than serving coffees to the envoys.[29]

In many ways, this type of diplomacy is just part of a wider strategy to increase American influence in the region through supporting allies, rather than adherence to traditions of diplomacy and mediation. At another level, it reveals a complete failure to recognise the dynamic created by the late upstream–early downstream development conundrum, plus the fact that upstreamers will not only develop water whilst it is in their country, but also that they are legally entitled do so. At yet another level, the unfaltering World Bank and US support for the Egyptian position reflects a willingness to accept a single country's hoarding of what is by definition an international resource so long as it meets their wider political agendas. Down by the riverside, it is the people of borderland Benishagul and Egyptian and Sudanese farmers who bear the consequences.

---

[28] Personal communication with an anonymous hydropolitical analyst, 2010.
[29] Personal communication with various hydropolitical analysts and water lawyers, 2018–2021.

Hoarding on the Jordan

The fate of many a Palestinian farmer is similarly determined by an international water agreement. We return to the Oslo II Agreement that the Palestine Liberation Organisation (PLO) signed with Israel in 1995, which codified water allocation that had been established following nearly three decades of Israeli occupation. This left the newly created Palestinian Authority control over only 10 per cent of the waters that flow within the West Bank and Gaza, from which the newly created Palestinian Water Authority has attempted to execute its hydraulic mission. Israel's hydraulic mission had been completed well beforehand, following the 1950s draining of the Huleh Marshes and the 1960s National Water Carrier that pumped water from the Lake of Tiberias down to the Negev/Naqab desert, making it bloom (a phenomenon described in Chapter 2).

Innovators in Israel have, in the meantime, perfected drip irrigation techniques and implemented world-class levels of wastewater reuse. The state has also built so many desalination plants that pure H_2O is being used to irrigate the desert after being remineralised (as we saw in Chapter 2 as well). Many in Israel now claim that it has more than enough water, is climate-proof, and can sell the manufactured or fresh water as a goodwill gesture to their Palestinian and Jordanian neighbours.[30]

Meanwhile, the Palestinian residents of the West Bank have less water available per capita in 2022 than when the Oslo Agreement was signed. In Gaza, desalination is too expensive for most, and with wastewater contaminating the groundwater, superbugs are mutating and creating a toxic 'biosphere of water'. (Chapter 3). Most of the water that Israel channels along its National Water Carrier from the Lake of Tiberias stops at the border of Gaza. Tantalisingly within the view of people in Gaza but very much out of their reach, the flows are reserved instead to grow potatoes and herbs which are exported to Europe.

Even if the Israeli state does not need so much water, the distribution of control over the transboundary flows remains a mirror reflection of the relative power between the rival states. Today, Israel controls more water than Jordan and the Palestinians combined, more than double its legal entitlement when measured against the principles of international water law.[31]

While farmers in Massafer Yatta (southern West Bank) harvested a poor yield of wheat in 2005, as shown in Figure 4.3, the industrial-scale agricultural schemes of Israeli settlements received a secure supply less than two kilometres away.

Decades of US mediation of Palestinian–Israeli negotiations have done nothing to change the hegemony of the arrangement. Though Palestinian negotiators

---

[30] Katz, 'Undermining demand management with supply management: Moral hazard in Israeli water policies.'
[31] Zeitoun et al., 'The Yarmouk tributary to the Jordan River II: Infrastructure impeding the transformation of equitable transboundary water arrangements,' and Zeitoun et al., 'The Yarmouk tributary to the Jordan River I: Agreements impeding equitable transboundary water arrangements.'

Figure 4.3 Farmers in Massafer Yatta (southern West Bank) harvesting a poor yield of wheat in 2005. This rainfed agriculture compares with the industrial-scale irrigation schemes of Israeli settlements a few hundred metres away.
Source: Author.

sought to base their position—and constructive talks—on the principles of international water law, their attempts proved futile. In 2001, at Camp David, the Palestinians were literally shoved aside by US mediators who offered to buy their way out of the mess. One of these erased the principles of water sharing that were being written on the whiteboard and replaced it with the simpler 'US = $' message. The US would fund all desalination plants necessary for the benefit of Israelis and Palestinians. This was a techno-fix par excellence if you can ignore its well-known drawbacks. During the last serious attempt to resurrect the Oslo negotiations, under US President George W. Bush, Jr in Annapolis, Maryland, in 2008, Israeli negotiators and American mediators alike pressed the water strategists to define precisely how much water was in the aquifers to negotiate—thereby setting for them the unending task of trying to decipher the movement of water throughout the Karst aquifers.

Meanwhile, the Palestinian–Israeli Joint Water Committee (JWC) that was established by the 1995 Oslo II Agreement proliferated. The Palestinian technicians, who had until then been working under the employment of the Israeli occupying authorities, were now hailed as equals by Israeli politicians and would join Israeli technicians in the field to measure water quality and water table levels in wells.

Seeing Israelis and Palestinians enjoying falafel together by a well proved a great opportunity to cement the optimism. It was a gushing moment for those who harboured liberal environmental peacebuilding hopes, and commentators doubled down on showcasing the 'cooperation' that water could bring. To the Palestinians seeking independence, the JWC looked a lot more like a vehicle of colonisation, as it did to analysts who actually looked at its outcomes. Even the World Bank saw the JWC as an obstacle to the development of the Palestinian state and called for its reform.[32] In seeking to build the water sector and improve the functioning of the JWC, the Palestinian minister of water withdrew from scheduled meetings around 2012. The move proved unpopular with donors, who would only fund Israel-approved projects through the JWC, but it did not stop the Israeli side from laying more water infrastructure for settlements. The lack of Palestinian control over the situation was exposed, JWC meetings were resumed, and they continue to this day.

When one understands that water conflict and cooperation coexist, one can accept that any water-related process can be like a wolf in sheep's clothing. If one can see the suffering caused by the conflict, one would then seek the appropriate pathway towards a resolution. In the case at hand, an analytical lens of political ecology[33] would be much more effective than a determinist 'water leads to peace' perspective or, worse still, treating the dynamics as a struggle between two states.[34]

The journal articles and grassroots activism that draw attention to the darker side of the transboundary water arrangement can appear cynical or defeatist when compared to the feel-good photo-ops that still linger as ripples in the wake of Oslo II. Environmental NGOs which promote cross-community water projects[35] have for decades attracted considerably more funds and attention than those who point to violations of the Human Right to Water in the West Bank[36] or of the Rules of War in Gaza.[37]

Any idea that there is parity in the processes is false, however, because of the way the message is delivered to the intended audience. Images of Israeli, Palestinian, and Jordanian mayors of Jordan River Valley villages holding hands seems to stick in some people's minds more than the plea of Palestinian mothers to be free to work their land. The optics are important, as no mediator is likely to hear that, per the agreement, the Palestinians were meant to develop their water sector with control over only one drop in every ten or that the Palestinian–Israeli JWC lubricates the ongoing colonisation of the West Bank. At least they did not when the Palestinian water negotiations team

---

[32] World Bank, 'West Bank and Gaza: Assessment of restrictions on Palestinian water sector development sector note April 2009'.

[33] With eyes wide open, and to much greater effect, Muna Dajani reaches for a lens of 'infrastructural violence' and so brings attention back down to those who suffer; see, e.g., Dajani (2020) and Dajani and Mason (2018).

[34] Zeitoun, *Power and Water*, chapter 4.

[35] Abitbol, *Hydropolitical Peacebuilding*.

[36] See reports by Human Rights Watch (2021) and the UN Human Rights Council (2021).

[37] Like Al Mezan et al., 'Joint urgent appeal to the United Nations special procedures on the escalating water and sanitation crisis in the Gaza Strip, occupied Palestinian territory'.

was being advised to employ international water law to resolve the water aspect of (much) wider political negotiations. By controlling the most water but needing it the least, Israel must choose to negotiate a fairer arrangement. But this will not happen in the context of extreme Zionism's chauvinism that legitimises the denial of basic human rights to Palestinians. A more equitable arrangement is unlikely to happen in a world where hoarding water by the more powerful state is not just normal but also is actively supported by the most powerful of mediators.

The rules for sharing water

Those who are keen to reduce the suffering caused by international water conflicts have their work cut out for them: cut through the misperceptions, overhaul the structures, reshape the political economy. Simple. Those involved in water diplomacy may aim a little lower and can choose to either ensure the conflicts do not become physically violent by maintaining the status quo (like the United States and World Bank did on the Jordan and Nile) or to push for an arrangement that looks a little bit fairer. The goal here should be 'transformation' and not 'conflict management', because the latter has become a euphemism for perpetuating the status quo.

Transforming a water conflict is an elusive goal. What seems fair to one state may seem unfair to another. And what seems fair to one state may be wildly unjust to some of those living in that state. Think of the Kurdish people opposed to the filling of the Ilisu Dam, the reservoir of which has risen a few feet since you first read about it at the start of this section. Similarly, what is fair today may not be fair a half century from now, when yet more dams have been built and more fields have been put into production.

In any case, 'fair' is a wholly subjective term. What does a 'fair' situation even look like? It is said that it is dead easy to tell what an unjust situation looks like, but difficult to define one that is wholly just. Similarly, unfair international water-sharing arrangements are easy to spot, but 'fair' ones are not. If there is no benchmark to measure what an unfair water-sharing arrangement looks like, then the whims of the more powerful side will usually prevail, helped along by politics of convenience.

Any water-sharing arrangement could be rationalised in a number of ways: allow one state to hoard all the watercourses within it (the so-called doctrine of *absolute territorial sovereignty*), divide up the water according to how much rainfall falls in each state, let the state that develops water first maintain that level of usage indefinitely, or follow the principles of international water law. Of these, international water law is by far the least bad.

Enter the lawyers. Critical thinkers know that law is made by the powerful, for the powerful, usually to preserve an order they have already established. As Anatole France said, 'the law in all of its majesty, forbids the rich as well as the poor from sleeping under bridges.' In many ways, international water law is no exception. It was spawned through the International Law Commission and International

Law Association, and its instruments and treaties read like a whistle-stop train-ride through colonial Europe: the 1911 Madrid Declaration, the 1956 Dubrovnik Statement, the 1961 Salzburg Resolution, the 1966 Helsinki Rules, the 1980 Belgrade Conference, the 1999 Campione Consolidation, and the 2004 Berlin Rules. The United States and Korea have had minimum influence but did pop up in the 1958 New York Resolution and the 1986 Seoul Rules, while Latin America, Africa, most of Asia, and the rest of the world have had none, apparently.

Still, a great number of states support international water law, and most of them are not the more powerful ones. The most common feature of countries that promote international water law is the will to improve the transboundary water arrangement that they find themselves in. The opposite is also true: countries that want to maintain or at best tweak the arrangements they have created often offer hostility towards international water law.

International water law was established after lawyers and engineers of the International Law Commission examined a wealth of work and precedence of state behaviour and coded it in 1997 as the Convention on the Non-Navigational Uses of International Watercourses, or 'the UN Watercourses Convention.'[38] The (relatively) multidisciplinary roots make international water law somewhat pragmatic. For example, the UN Water Convention grapples directly with the inevitable tension created by late-developing upstream states and the harm that will be produced on the downstream states. Importantly, the UN Water Convention acknowledges that upstream development of water sources will impact downstreamers, but that upstream states are legally entitled to do so, and that—as the very astute former Special Rapporteur of the Commission Steve McCaffrey never tires to point out—some harm is inevitable, but that harm must not be 'significant.' What, then, is 'significant'?

The Watercourses Convention is equally pragmatic when it comes to guiding allocations of water. It asserts that the custom that has developed is one of 'equitable and reasonable use' of watercourses. That is, the legal entitlement of a state to a transboundary watercourse should be a result of deliberations that consider the economic dependency of each state on the watercourse in question, as well as established uses, the amount of people using it, and access to alternative sources, amongst other factors.

The Watercourses Convention is of course subject to the same weaknesses as IHL, and indeed, all international law. It does little to deter state actions, because violations go without consequence. Today, however, the Gabčíkovo–Nagymaros and the Uruguayan–Paraguayan Pulp Mills cases have benefited from handling in the International Court of Justice, dozens of lawyers working for or associated with the UN Economic Commission for Europe (UNECE) secretariat promote international water law around the world, and its principles are being employed regularly (as on the Nile). The hope is that the more codes are written and followed, the more the ideas become norms—just as human slavery was considered unconscionable in many circles

---

[38] United Nations (UN), '12. Convention on the Law of the Non-Navigational Uses of International Watercourses.'

before states made it illegal. The hope is that the next generation sees as outrageous an 85–15 per cent split of any river rather than acceptable like their predecessors (us) do.

But there remains visceral opposition to international water law. This is precisely because it challenges the status quo established by the earlier developing and more powerful states. One only has to look at which states have not signed on to the Convention to identify those that would like to change the current arrangement.[39] States which prefer the status quo—the United States, Egypt, Israel, Turkey—are not likely to sign up soon. Indeed, in his response to a campaign to get the United Kingdom to ratify the UN Watercourses Convention, the head of the UK Department for International Development Hilary Benn argued in 2008 that 'none of the large (geographically and/or economically) countries that share water with their neighbours (Brazil, China, Egypt, India, and Israel) ... have acceded to the Convention.' The United Kingdom changed its position only a few years later, just as Egypt did when the balance of power changed. And if the international water law is used as guide, it may eventually become a norm that would be more difficult to transgress. Are we heading to a world where hoarding water is no longer tolerated? I hope so, but aspirations are not enough.

---

[39] 'Status of the Watercourses Convention,' International Water Law Project.

Conclusion

Water Whilst It Is in Our Hands

> We will not know our own injustice if we cannot imagine justice. We will not be free if we do not imagine freedom.
>
> —Ursula K. Le Guin[1]

A lake revealing very little of what lurks underneath.

Source: Author.

At the outset of this book, I posited that if we do not challenge our assumptions about water, we will continue to desecrate water's essential qualities and that understanding water is the best first step to take. I asserted that many of us like to think that water is a

---

[1] Le Guin, A War Without End, 3.

precious resource, that we think we use it to cleanse, nourish, and unify but, in fact, we treat it like a shoddy throwaway. The apparent paradox is readily explained by ignorance: we do not understand how water shapeshifts around our world so we develop unfounded ideas about how we use it. We insist on turning off the tap when brushing our teeth but do not consider how many thousands of times more water is 'used' to produce the hamburger we ate for lunch. We forget that water is constantly replenishing itself and too often assume we are always just about to run out or be flooded. We blame water scarcity on nature or climate change, remaining blissfully ignorant of the fact that the much more important driver is what *we* decide to do with water.

We manage water under the constraints imposed by very well-established political and economic structures. Within the logic created by these structures, everything we do is sensible. It is pragmatic to use every drop we can to irrigate deserts and export fresh vegetables; it is practical to pay two thousand times more than we need to for tap water wrapped in plastic; it is perfectly rational to turn wetlands—the second most biodiverse spots on earth—into sugar plantations so that we can produce soft drinks, wrap them in plastic, and feed them to our kids—and then make sure they turn the tap off when they scrape it off their teeth. When the demand for water outstrips the supply, we dig more wells and build more dams. We reach for the sea, catch clouds, dig deeper wells, build more and bigger dams, and then cover their reservoirs in plastic. We marshal our most creative minds, souls, and technology to do anything apart from reducing that demand. Or even questioning whether we should.

Our collective ingenuity has enabled us to harness water so effectively that civilisation has the space to flourish. States use that knowledge as they embark on their hydraulic missions to satisfy, pacify, or flush-out the local people. Some governments then hand over the infrastructure they have built to private companies so that any profit made leaves the country as quickly as foreign contractors do when the conditions they had been promised no longer exist. As during war. When thirst outweighs the risk of catching a bullet, we turn our long-range rifles to water points and hunt people like gazelles at a pond. We use rivers to flood our enemies or hide mass murder. We shoot up public water reservoirs or throw grandfathers down wells so that those we have forced from their homes will not return. When denied or used in these ways, water is a source of thirst and of terror. Through all this, we are not even aware of those who have risked and given their lives to restore water to your taps or clean out the wells. This water no longer nourishes: it becomes the carrier of disease so awful that no media anywhere will show its victims as their liquid insides empty out. In particularly long wars, the impact of attacks reverberate in such a way that the quality of water degrades to the point that micro-plastics or ecological health are the least of all possible concerns. Water becomes a carrier of the microorganisms that mutate to resist otherwise life-saving antibiotics. The more we drink of this tainted water, the more likely we are to die from the infection than the bullet that caused it. The cycle continues. The more we treat water just as stuff, the less we understand it, and the more we abuse it.

Within this logic, it is little surprise to see powerful states hoarding water. Governments decide to develop the rain that falls within their political borders, as if it was static like the political borders they have sovereignty over. Those decisions force farming families in the less powerful downstream states into miserable situations that are readily overlooked. The more we tolerate other states doing the same, the more we legitimise the denial of what every human should enjoy. Yet norms of fair water-sharing are unfashionable in the current geopolitical climate and are ignored by diplomats who would rather manage than transform international water conflicts.

In the sense that we are totally locked into the systems that we develop, we are like spiders caught in our own web. Hydrocycles always outlive human life cycles, and certainly electoral cycles. Challenging the dominant structures that shape our decisions can be career suicide, so we adapt. In adapting, we render the structures themselves more resilient by accommodating them and ceding our own power until we have no more sway over the outcomes than a leaf floating on a stream.

Water is unending, we have the means to use it sustainably, but we remain very thirsty. Still, somehow, many of us deny that we do all this. The depth of our self-delusion is stunning. The ignorance is not just blissful—it is sublime. The myopic observer might argue that what water reflects about humanity is our lack of concern for cleansing, nourishment, and unification and the depths of our greed and chauvinism. Perhaps my grandchildren will become snipers and wait for your grandchildren to approach the water tap stands. Maybe your children will become lawyers who interpret International Humanitarian Law to legalise the targeting of water treatment plants. It is possible that my nieces will be writing clever clauses in international agreements to preserve the lion's share of water for their own country, while your nephews chant in demonstrations against bad dams, for more sharing or less hoarding. For all we know, we all shall continue to trust the advertisers who tell us there is no better way to provide good water to poor children in slums and villages than to drink the water they have taken from mountain springs. Most probably the bulk of us will continue to eat asparagus and drink the cola that ruins someone else's water source elsewhere in the world. Too many of us will continue to cling to our romantic beliefs about water as tightly as we maintain our habits which abuse the very same. This means we will carry on ignoring arguments and evidence that challenge our beliefs because, in those rare instances that we think about changing the path we are on, we will retreat to justifications like 'my country and my people, first!' or shrug that 'it's out of our hands.' Like leaves floating on a stream.

Meaning that this explanation to the apparent paradox—commodify, ignore, abuse—is watertight.

Except that it's not. The explanation is in fact quite leaky. Hundreds of holes have been blown into the paradox by hundreds of thousands of people who challenge the cynicism.

I am not suddenly seeing the glass half-full through rose-coloured glasses. I am merely reflecting on what I have observed (but not dwelled upon): that an overwhelming amount of thoughtful ingenuity and care flies alongside all the abuse.

People who reconnect with water provide us with hope because they assume that we can seize or create opportunities to change things. These are the people who help us reflect on what we do with water. They are the ones who think critically, challenge received wisdom, bust the myths, teach water better, manage water more sensibly, and undermine or work around the logic set out by the political economy of water. These people are the rain.

The growers know water better than anyone and have the most to teach. Their understanding of the cost and value of the water they depend on for their livelihoods is vital to everybody's quality of life. Primary school teachers help kids understand that they are drinking dinosaur pee or adapt Western American water-cycle diagrams to their local contexts. High school teachers probe teenagers to find out where the water goes when they flush the toilet. College and university professors inspire new ways to clean up the waste, and some even explain why so much waste is not even treated in the first place. Teachers at all levels help others learn that water scarcity is, more often than not, artificial, and that anthropogenic climate change can sometimes be used as a very convenient truth twisted to absolve us from action.

In their wake swim the thousands of students who take the risk to research topics no one has ever conceived of, to better understand water. They will teach us how to read so much of the world from a puddle or a ripple; to use the latest technology to discover that water actually has a phase beyond liquid, solid, or vapour; or to explore the newest frontier by integrating this kind of grounded knowledge into the realms of politics and society.

Raise a glass to all the parents who get their children to question where water comes from, where it goes, and what it nourishes or cleanses along the way. In so doing, they instil a sense of duty to and a gracious respect for the environment and others. They teach us not only to waste less water but they also compel us all to reflect on *how* we use water, on *what we do with it for those moments that it is in our hands*.

This is not about stewardship over a resource. Water is so much more interesting than a thing to cherish and protect. Besides, while we may be able to watch over some water bodies, the cyclical movement of water is complex and elusive—and shuns total control by any of us. This is about realising that water is us, and then sticking to convictions and principles—even when every incentive, every book, every directive, and most friends tell us to do otherwise. The thinking required goes well beyond using multiple disciplines; it requires blending them to the point that the boundaries are no longer distinguishable. The actions required are as clear as a healthy chalk stream. When we restore a river, push for alternatives to bad dams, protect water from the dogs of war, and call for clean-ups and new ways of thinking, we shed our privilege and gain agency in ways that those who conform exceptionally well to the established political economic structures may never understand.

We should build monuments to those who have risked or given their lives to deliver water to others by wading through live ammunition to repair pumping stations. To lawyers who apply their craft to safeguard water systems during war or to open doors for more effective cooperation over international watercourses. To others who sacrifice their careers by speaking against their municipality or water company when it turns the taps of others off, or risk prison by turning the taps back on under the cover of darkness. Many more resist the commodification of water in more head-on ways, by pushing for their country to legislate water rights for everyone and not letting up the pressure so that the right is enforced. Those who so guide the flow of water are restoring dignity and a basic standard of living for others. These are the lions who challenge the cynical explanation that I've offered with something much more creative: hope for a way out. They are ready to teach if we are ready to learn. The next book will be about them.

In the spirit of avoiding easy answers, I hope you question my response to the monotonous mantra 'water is life.' My pessimistic self has not been able to say much more than 'water is death, too.' Not very deep. A much better answer comes from those who are able to think contrapuntally, like Professor Aimée Craft: 'Water is life ... has so many expressions but really if you think about it in the [Anishinaabe] language—nibi onje biimaadiiziiwin—it is water because of life, but life because of water. We have water so we can have life, and we have life because we have water.... Does that make sense?'[2]

It makes no sense if you were trained to think that your job is to restore or preserve nature for the good of humanity, as I was. Understanding water-is-life-is-water makes loads of sense, however, if you think the relationship we have with water should not be one of exploitation dictated by short-term interests, but one of harmony—and founded within a sense of our place within the world we are part of, to paraphrase philosopher Souleymane Bachir Diagne's words uttered from the banks of the Senegal River.

At this point in world history, many of us who are schooled in the mainstream systems seek to liberate our minds, to change the way we see and use water, to recognise where we are within the water cycle, or to see rain for what it is. Such acts challenge those who exert influence over us. Which makes me think that political, technological, or social progress and caring about water are one and the same thing. In this sense, thinking more deeply about the abstract—some would say essential—qualities of water is one of the most consequential things you can do for the rest of the world or for your own life. For together this can build into an informed and caring ethos of water—a culture of respect based on a thoughtful understanding of water and just how clearly our use of it reflects our souls and egos.

As we work towards that goal, how and what does the critical mirror reflect on us in the meantime? At the broadest level, and a quarter of the way through the twenty-first century, water reveals just how regressive is the era we are living. Social progress appears limited to too few individuals in wealthy democracies, kingdoms, or dictatorships, and environmental progress is constrained to preserving or restoring those bits of the environment and bodies of water that they can exploit. Advances in politics

---

[2] Gray, 'Decolonizing water: A conversation with Aimée Craft.'

comes more from people's actions than through political structures but reveal that we remain nonetheless stuck in a cycle that can at best bring us forward to a point many of us thought we has passed several decades ago. Technological innovations are exhilarating to contemplate and will be broadly beneficial if the ethics are intelligently and compassionately debated and acted upon. For all the reasons outlined in this book, we will not extend the benefits of any and all such achievements to other people living in other ways, along other rivers—until we, too, are the rain, until we harmonise our own selves with water's abstract and beautiful qualities.

Bibliography

Abbara, Aula, Omar Zakieh, Diana Rayes, Simon M. Collin, Naser Almhawish, Richard Sullivan, Ibrahim Aladhan, Maia Tarnas, Molly Whalen-Browne, Maryam Omar, Ahmad Tarakji, and Nabil Karah. 2021. 'Weaponizing water as an instrument of war in Syria: Impact on diarrhoeal disease in Idlib and Aleppo governorates,' *International Journal of Infectious Diseases*, 108: 202–208.

Abitbol, E. 2013. *Hydropolitical Peacebuilding: Israeli-Palestinian Water Relations and the Transformation of Asymmetric Conflict in the Middle East.* PhD thesis published by the University of Bradford.

Abu Sitta, Salman. 2011. *An Atlas of Palestine*. London: Palestine Lands Society.

Ahmed, Iman. 2013. *Merowe Dam in Northern Sudan: A Case of Population Displacement and Impoverishment*. American University of Cairo. https://link.springer.com.

Al-Madhhachi, Abdul-Sahib T., Khayyun A. Rahi, and Wafa K. Leabi. 2020. 'Hydrological Impact of Ilisu Dam on Mosul Dam: The River Tigris,' *Geosciences*, 10(4): 120. https://doi.org/10.3390/geosciences10040120.

Al Mezan, Al Haq, CIHRS, and Habitat International. 2020. 'Joint urgent appeal to the United Nations Special Procedures on the escalating water and sanitation crisis in the Gaza Strip, occupied Palestinian territory.' Gaza City, Al Mezan Center for Human Rights, Al-Haq—Law in the Service of Man, Cairo Institute for Human Rights Studies, Habit International Coalition—Housing and Land Rights Network.

al-Sabouni, Marwa. 2016. *The Battle for Home: The Memoir of a Syrian Architect*. London: Thames & Hudson.

Al-Saidi, Mohammad, Emma Lauren Roach, and Bilal Ahmed Hassen Al-Saeedi. 2020. 'Conflict resilience of water and energy supply infrastructure: Insights from Yemen,' *Water*, 12(11): 3269.

Alatout, S. 2006. 'Towards a bio-territorial conception of power: Territory, population, and environmental narratives in Palestine and Israel,' *Political Geography*, 25: 601–621.

Alatout, S. 2009. 'Bringing abundance into environmental politics: Constructing a Zionist network of water abundance, immigration and colonization,' *Social Studies of Science*, 39: 363–394.

Allan, J. A. 2001. *The Middle East Water Question: Hydropolitics and the Global Economy*. London: I. B. Tauris.

Allan, Tony. 2011. *Virtual Water: Tackling the Threat to Our Planet's Most Precious Resource.* London: I. B. Tauris.

Allouche, Jeremy. 2019. 'State building, nation making and post-colonial hydropolitics in India and Israel: Visible and hidden forms of violence at multiple scales,' *Political Geography*, 75:102051. https://doi.org/10.1016/j.polgeo.2019.102051.

Allouche, Jeremy. 2018. 'Desalination has a waste problem.' Circle of Blue website. https://www.circleofblue.org/2019/world/desalination-has-a-waste-problem/.

Altaher A. M., E. S. Abdul Ghafoor, W. I. Amudi, et al. 2016. 'Comparative identification of bacterial quality in liquid soap between Nasser and European Gaza hospitals, Khanyounis Governorate,' *Asian Journal of Pharmacy, Nursing and Medical Sciences*, 4(5): 77–83.

Amichai, Yehuda. 2000. 'Once I wrote now and in other days: Thus glory passes, thus pass the psalms,' in *Open Closed Open: Poems*, trans. by Chana Bloch and Chana Kronfeld. New York: Harcourt, 29–36.

Bibliography

Anderson, Michael, dir. 1955. *The Dam Busters* [motion picture]. Hertfordshire: Associated British Picture Corporation.

Auden, W. H. 1957. "The More Loving One."

Blackbourn, David. 2007. *The Conquest of Nature: Water, Landscape and the Making of Modern Germany.* London: Pimlico.

Butt, G. 2009. *Life at the Crossroads: A History of Gaza.* Limassol, Cyprus: Rimal Publications.

Cascão, Ana Elisa. 2009. 'Changing power relations in the Nile river basin: Unilateralism vs. cooperation?,' *Water Alternatives,* 2: 245–268.

Cascão, Ana Elisa, and Alan Nicol. 2016. 'GERD: ANew norms of cooperation in the Nile Basin?,' *Water International,* 41: 550–573.

Cassini, Alessandro, Liselotte Diaz Högberg, Diamantis Plachouras et al. 2019. 'Attributable deaths and disability-adjusted life-years caused by infections with antibiotic-resistant bacteria in the EU and the European Economic Area in 2015: A population-level modelling analysis,' *Lancet Infectious Diseases,* 19: 56–66.

Chomsky, Noam. 1993, October. 'The Israel–Arafat agreement,' *Z Magazine.* https://chomsky.info.

Clark Howard, Brian. 2015. 'Why did L.A. drop 96 million "shade balls" into its water?' *National Geographic.* https://nationalgeographic.com.

Clot, Ziyad. 2010. *Il n'y aura pas d'état Palestinien: Journal d'un négociateur en Palestine.* Paris: Max Milo.

CO. 1926. 'Agreement as to water concession at Jerusalem, between the Crown Agents for the Colonies and Euripides Mavrommatis.' London: UK National Archives Commonwealth Office record CAOG 14/124.

CO. 1927. 'Draft agreement 13th October 1927 between Field Marshall the Right Honourable Herbert Charles Onslow and the Jaffa Electric Company Limited.' London: UK National Archives Commonwealth Office record CO 733/134/6.

CO. 1938. 'Irrigation and settlement in Southern Palestine.' Miscellaneous correspondence and reports from the Commonwealth Office, including 'Notes on the Negeb, Palestine's Empty Half.' London: UK National Archives Commonwealth Office record CO 733/380/8.

Coca-Cola and The Nature Conservancy. 2010. 'Product water footprint assessments: Practical application in corporate water stewardship.' Coca-Cola Enterprise, The Nature Conservancy, The Water Footprint Network. https://www.conservationgateway.org/Documents/TCCC-TNC%20footprint%20report.pdf.

Conker, Ahmet. 2014. *An Enhanced Notion of Power for Inter-state and Transnational Hydropolitics: An Analysis of Turkish-Syrian Water Relations and the Ilisu Dam.* Doctoral thesis, University of East Anglia.

Dajani, Muna. 2020. 'Thirsty water carriers: The production of uneven waterscapes in Sahl al-Battuf,' *Contemporary Levant,* 5: 97–112.

Dajani, Muna, and Michael Mason. 2018. 'Counter-infrastructure as resistance in the hydro-social territory of the occupied Golan Heights,' in *Water, Technology, and the Nation-State,* edited by Filippo Menga and Erik Swyngedouw. London: Routledge, 114–130.

Daoudy, Marwa. 2020. *The Origins of the Syrian Conflict: Climate Change and Human Security.* Cambridge: Cambridge University Press.

Darwish, M. 1995. *Memory for Forgetfulness: August, Beirut, 1982.* Berkeley: University of California Press.

Dawood, Ismal. 2019. 'Does the memorandum of understanding in water management between Turkey and Iraq guarantee Iraq its water rights?' *Water Forum.* Save the Tigris. https://www.savethetigris.org/does-the-memorandum-of-understanding-in-water-management-between-turkey-and-iraq-guarantee-iraq-its-water-rights/

de Albuquerque, Catarina. 2014. *Realising the Human Rights to Water and Sanitation: A Handbook by the UN Special Rapporteur.* Portugal: UN Special Rapporteur.

Delli-Priscoli, Jerome. 2001. 'Participation, river basin organizations and flood management.' Presented at Workshop on Strengthening Capacity in Participatory Planning and Management for Flood Mitigation and Preparedness in Large River Basins, 20–23 November 2001, Bangkok, Thailand. Water and Mineral Resources Section, Environment and Natural Resources Development Division, Economic and Social Commission for Asia and the Pacific.

Dewachi, Omar. 2015. 'When wounds travel,' *Medicine Anthropology Theory*, 2: 61–82.

Digg. 2020. 'A German waterworks marketed their bottled tap water to the French city of Evian and their reactions were priceless.' Digg. https://digg.com/video/german-tap-water-comes-to-evian.

Dirar, Azza. 2021. *Valuing Property in the Manasir Communities Near the Merowe Dam*. PhD thesis published by the University of East Anglia.

Dureab, Fekri, Khalid Shibib, Yazoumé Yé, Albrecht Jahn, and Olaf Müller. 2018. 'Cholera epidemic in Yemen,' *Lancet Global Health*, 6(12): E1283.

Fallon, Amy L., Bruce A. Lankford, and Derek Weston. 2021. 'Navigating wicked water governance in the "solutionscape" of science, policy, practice, and participation,' *Ecology and Society*, 26(2): article 37.

FCO. 1979. 'Jordan waters.' In Correspondence between Foreign and Commonwealth Office and Embassy in Amman. London: UK National Archives Commonwealth Office record FCO93-1988, RRM040/1.

Felton, Ryan. 2020. 'How Coke and Pepsi make millions from bottling tap water, as residents face shutoffs.' *Consumer Reports*, 10 July. https://www.consumerreports.org/bottled-water/how-coke-and-pepsi-make-millions-from-bottling-tap-water-as-residents-face-shutoffs/.

'Flint water crisis,' Wikipedia. https://en.wikipedia.org/wiki/Flint_water_crisis.

Fewtrell, Lorna, Rachel B. Kaufmann, David Kay, Wayne Enanoria, Laurence Haller, and John M. Colford. 2005. 'Water, sanitation, and hygiene interventions to reduce diarrhoea in less developed countries: A systematic review and meta-analysis,' *Lancet Infectious Diseases*, 5: 42–52.

Finkelstein, Norman. 1995. *Image and Reality of the Israel-Palestine Conflict*. New York: Verso.

Forsyth, T. 2003. *Critical Political Ecology: The Politics of Environmental Science*. London: Routledge.

Gooley, T. 2015. *How to Read Water: Clues, Signs & Patterns from Puddles to the Sea*. London: Sceptre/Hodder & Stoughton Ltd.

GC15. 2002. 'Substantive issues arising in the implementation of the International Covenant on Economic, Social and Cultural Rights, general comment 15 (Draft).' Geneva: UN Economic and Social Council, Committee on Economic, Social and Cultural Rights, Twenty-ninth session. https://digitallibrary.un.org/record/486454?ln=en.

GIZ. 2018. 'Yemen water sector: Damage assessment report of twelve water supply and sanitation local corporations (LC) and their affiliated branch offices and utilities: Stage III. Part 2: Situation assessment report and development of technical assistance and investment plans for the infrastructure rehabilitation of water supply and sanitation services. Annex 2: Technical assessment report for LC Aden.' Deutsche Gesellschaft für Internationaled Zusammenarbeit (GIZ) GmbH. https://www.giz.de/de/downloads/giz2021-en-yemen-water-sector-stage-3-part-1.pdf.

Gleick, Peter H., and Meena Palaniappan. 2010. 'Peak water limits to freshwater withdrawal and use,' *Proceedings of the National Academy of Sciences of the USA*, 107: 11155–11162.

Gleick, Peter H. 2010. *Bottled and Sold: The Story Behind Our Obsession with Bottled Water*. London: Island Press.

Goma Epidemiology Group. 2005. 'Public health impact of Rwandan refugee crisis: What happened in Goma, Zaire, in July, 1994?,' *Lancet*, 345: 339–344.

Gray, C. 2018. 'Decolonizing water: A conversation with Aimée Craft.' Centre for International Governance Innovation. https://www.cigionline.org/articles/decolonizing-water-conversation-aimee-craft/

Greco, Francesca. 2013. 'Hegemony and counter-hegemony in virtual water trade: Justice for indigenous people?' Presented at Sixth International Workshop on Hydro-Hegemony. 12–13 January 2013, London UEA Water Security Research Centre/London Water Research Group. UK NATIONAL ARCHIVES REF WO 252/1378.

GSI (Geological Survey of Israel). 1943. *Water resources of Palestine*. G.S.I., H.Q. Palestine.

Gyawali, Dipak. 2001. *Rivers, Technology and Society: Learning the Lessons of Water Management in Nepal*. London: Zed Books.

Harvey, David. 2000. *Space of Hope*. Edinburgh: Edinburgh University Press.

Hays, James B. 1948. 'T.V.A. on the Jordan: Proposals for irrigation and hydro-electric development in Palestine.' A report prepared under the auspices of the Commission on Palestine Surveys, Public Affairs Press, assisted by A. E. Barrekette, with an introduction by Walter C. Lowdermilk. Washington, DC.

Heming, Li, Paul Waley, and Phil Rees. 2001. 'Reservoir resettlement in China: Past experience and the Three Gorges Dam,' *Geographical Journal*, 167: 195–212.

Hepworth, Nick, Julio C. Postigo, and Bruno Güemes Delgado. 2010. *Drop by Drop: A Case Study of Peruvian Asparagus and the Impacts of the UK's Water Footprint*. London: Progressio, in association with Centro Peruano De Estudios Sociales, and Water Witness International.

Higgins, Polly, Damien Short, and Nigel South. 2013. 'Protecting the planet: A proposal for a law of ecocide,' *Crime, Law and Social Change*, 59: 251–266.

Hiorth, Albert. 1938. 'Plan for the restoration of the Near East in the light of biblical prophecies (Gen. 15,18 Isa.19, 23-24).' London: UK National Archives Commonwealth Office record CO 733/355/13.

Hourani, Albert. 1991. *A History of the Arab Peoples*. New York: Warner Books.

Hulme, Mike. 2020. 'One Earth, many futures, no destination,' *One Earth*, 2: 309–311.

Human Rights Watch (HRW). 2021. 'A threshold crossed: Israeli authorities and the crimes of apartheid and persecution.' Human Rights Watch. https://www.hrw.org/report/2021/04/27/threshold-crossed/israeli-authorities-and-crimes-apartheid-and-persecution.

Hunter, Paul R., Alan M. MacDonald, and Richard C. Carter. 2010. 'Water supply and health,' *Plos One*, 7(11): e1000361. https://doi.org/10.1371/journal.pmed.1000361.

Hunter, Paul R., Denis Zmirou-Navier, and Philippe Hartemann. 2009. 'Estimating the impact on health of poor reliability of drinking water interventions in developing countries,' *Science of the Total Environment*, 407: 2621–2624.

Hutton, G., and M. Varughese. 2016. *The Costs of Meeting the 2030 Sustainable Development Goal Targets on Drinking Water, Sanitation, and Hygiene*. Washington, DC: Water and Sanitation Program of the World Bank Group.

ICRC. 2015. *Urban Services During Protracted Armed Conflict: A Call for a Better Approach to Assisting Affected People*. Geneva: International Committee of the Red Cross.

IHA. 2019. *Hydropower Sector Climate Resilience Guide*. London: International Hydropower Association.

IRJWC. 1907. *Souvenir Album of the Holy Land, with Exceptionally Rare Views of the Sacred River Jordan*. New York: International River Jordan Water Company.

Jobbins, Guy, Jack Kalpakian, Abdelouahid Chriyaa, Ahmed Legroun, and El Houssine El Mzouri. 2015. 'To what end? Drip irrigation and the water-energy-food nexus in Morocco,' *International Journal of Water Resources Development*, 3(1): 1–9.

Johnson, Steven. 2006. *The Ghost Map: The Story of London's Most Terrifying Epidemic—and How It Changed Science, Cities, and the Modern World*. London: Penguin Books.

Katz, David. 2016. 'Undermining demand management with supply management: Moral hazard in Israeli water policies,' *Water*, 8(4), 159. https://doi.org/10.3390/w8040159

Keys, P. W., R. J. van der Ent, L. J. Gordon, H. Hoff, R. Nikoli, and H. H. G. Savenije. 2012. 'Analyzing precipitationsheds to understand the vulnerability of rainfall dependent regions,' *Biogeosciences*, 9: 733–746.

Kingsolver, B. 2010. 'Fresh Water Issues,' *National Geographic Magazine*, April 2010.

Lamba, M., D. W. Graham, and S. Z. Ahammad. 2017. 'Hospital wastewater releases of carbapenem-resistance pathogens and genes in urban India,' *Environmental Science and Technology*, 51: 13906–13912.

Lankford, Bruce, Alvar Closas, James Dalton, Elena López Gunn, Tim Hess, Jerry W. Knox, Saskia van der Kooij, Jonathan Lautze, David Molden, Stuart Orr, Jamie Pittock, Brian Richter, Philip J. Riddell, Christopher A. Scott, Jean-philippe Venot, Jeroen Vos, and Margreet Zwarteveen. 2020. 'A scale-based framework to understand the promises, pitfalls and paradoxes of irrigation efficiency to meet major water challenges,' *Global Environmental Change*, 65. https://doi.org/10.1016/j.gloenvcha.2020.102182.

Lankford, B. 2018. 'Environmental Assessment for the proposed drip irrigation of Gabiro Commercial Farms Project (GCFP) in Nyagatare District, Eastern Province—Kenya.' Report Prepared for the Kenyan Ministry of Agriculture and Animal Resources (MINAGRI).

Laville, Sandra. 2020. 'England's privatised water firms paid £57bn in dividends since 1991,' *The Guardian*, 1 July 2020. https://www.theguardian.com/environment/2020/jul/01/england-privatised-water-firms-dividends-shareholders.

Le Guin, U. K. 2004. *A War Without End: The Wave in the Mind: Talks and Essays on the Writer, the Reader, and the Imagination*. Boulder, CO: Shambhala.

Linton, Jamie. 2010. *What Is Water?: The History of a Modern Abstraction*. Vancouver: University of British Columbia Press.

Llamosas, Cecilia, and Benjamin K. Sovacool. 2021. 'The future of hydropower? A systematic review of the drivers, benefits and governance dynamics of transboundary dams,' *Renewable and Sustainable Energy Reviews*, 137. https://doi.org/10.1016/j.rser.2020.110495.

Mann, Jonathan, Ernest Drucker, Daniel Tarantola, and Mary Pat McCabe. 1994. 'Bosnia: The war against public health,' *Medicine & Global Survival*, 1: 130–146.

Marks, William E. 2001. *The Holy Order of Water: Healing Earth's Waters and Ourselves*. Great Barrington: Bell Pond Books.

Masterman, E. W. G. 1908. 'The Upper Jordan River Valley,' *The Biblical World*, 32: 302–313.

McCaffrey, Stephen. 2005. 'The human right to water revisited,' in *Water and International Economic Law*, edited by Edith Brown Weiss, Laurence Boisson deChazournes, and Nathalie Bernasconi-Osterwalder. Oxford: Oxford University Press.

McCraken, Melissa. 2022. *Defining Effective Transboundary Water Cooperation*. London: Routledge.

McCully, Patrick. 2001. *Silenced Rivers: The Ecology and Politics of Large Dams* (enlarged and updated edition). London: Zed Books.

Menga, Filippo. 2016. 'Domestic and international dimensions of transboundary water politics,' *Water Alternatives*, 9(3): 704–733.

Menga, Filippo. 2018. *Power and Water in Central Asia*. Abingdon: Routledge.

Menga, Filippo, and Naho Mirumachi. 2016. 'Fostering Tajik hydraulic development: Examining the role of soft power in the case of the Rogun Dam.' *Water Alternatives*, 9(2): 373–388.

Messerschmid, Clemens. 2008. 'Palestinian and Zionist "prior use": Establishing the record of historic water use, 1920–1948.' Ramallah: Report prepared for Adam Smith International.

Mirumachi, Naho. 2015. *Transboundary Water Politics in the Developing World*. London: Routledge.

Mitchell, T. 2002. *Rule of Experts: Egypt, Techno-Politics, and Modernity*. London: University of California Press.

Molle, Francois, and Phillipe Floch. 2008. 'The "desert bloom" syndrome: Irrigation development, politics, and ideology in the Northeast of Thailand.' Mekong Program on Water, Environment and Resilience, Institut de Recherche pour le Développement, International Water Management Institute. MPOWER, Chiang Mai, Thailand.

Murakami, H. 2017. *Killing Commendatore*. New York: Alfred A. Knopf.

Musgrave, Paul. 'The beautiful, dumb dream of McDonald's Peace Theory: In the rich, lazy, and happy 1990s, Americans imagined a world that could be just like them.' *Foreign Policy*, November 26, 2020.

Nembrini, P. Giorgio. 1994. 'Lebanon: Water supply problems during the 1989 and 1990 wars.' in *Water and War: Symposium on Water in Armed Conflict, Montreux, 21–23 November 1994*, edited by ICRC. Geneva: International Committee of the Red Cross, 32–36.

Nembrini, P. Giorgio. 1995. 'Do water production and treatment facilities need greater protection in armed conflicts?' in *Water and War: Symposium on Water in Armed Conflicts*, edited by International Committee of the Red Cross. Geneva: International Committee of the Red Cross, 80–88.

Nembrini, P. Giorgio. 2000. *Cities in War: Thirsty Cities, Dili (East Timor)*. Geneva: Geneva Foundation.

Nembrini, P. Giorgio. 2001a. 'Huambo (Angola): Water supply in a war torn town: Evolution and impact of the different interventions since 1985,' in *Cities in War: Thirsty Cities, Occasional Paper No. 3*. Geneva: Geneva Foundation.

Nembrini, P. Giorgio. 2001b. 'Novi Sad (Republic of Yugoslavia): How the water supply of the town was affected by the NATO campaign of 1999,' in *Cities in War: Thirsty Cities, Occasional Paper No. 5*. Geneva: Geneva Foundation.

Nembrini, P. Giorgio. 2002. 'Monitoring of urban growth of Informal Settlements (IS) and population estimation from aerial photography and satellite imaging,' in *Cities in War: Thirsty Cities, Occasional Paper No. 6*. Geneva: Geneva Foundation.

Nembrini, P. Giorgio. 2010. 'The Gaza strip: The state of the water supply after the 2008–2009 war.' Occasional Paper No. 10.

Nembrini, P. Giorgio, C. Generelli, A. Al-Attar, M. A. Graf, A.M. Yousif, N. S. Karomy, H. M. Al Al-Fakhri, J. Abdul-Zehra, N. S. Alyas, and K. H. Al-Shakarchi. 2003. *Basrah Water Supply During the War on Iraq*. Geneva: Geneva Foundation and International Committee of the Red Cross.

Nembrini, P. Giorgio, C. Smith, A. Petters, R. Conti, and P. Smets. 2001. *Cities in War: Thirsty Cities, Monrovia (Liberia). Water Supply for Monrovia During and After the Civil War*. Geneva: Geneva Foundation.

Nembrini, Pier Giorgio, P. Jansen, J. F. Pinera, R. Luff, O. Bernard, M. Weber, and M. J. Elliot. 2002. 'Kabul water supply: Evolution since the 1992–94 civil war,' in *Cities in War: Thirsty Cities, Occasional Paper No. 7*. Geneva: Geneva Foundation.

Newton, Joshua. 2014. *'Water, Water Everywhere, Nor Any Drop to Drink': An Exploration of the Lack of a Formal Global Water Governance Regime*. Medford, MA: Tufts University Press.

Norman, Emma S. 2012. 'Cultural politics and transboundary resource governance in the Salish Sea,' *Water Alternatives*, 5: 138–160.

Nicolson, Helen J. 2011. 'Water in medieval warfare,' in *A History of Water Series II, Volume 3: Water, Geopolitics, and the New World Order*, edited by Terje Tvedt, Graham Chapman, and Roar Hagen. London: I. B. Tauris.

Nohle, Ellen, and Isabel Robinson. 2017. 'War in cities: The "reverberating effects" of explosive weapons,' in *Humanitarian Law & Policy*. Geneva: International Committee of the Red Cross. https://blogs.icrc.org/law-and-policy/2017/03/02/war-in-cities-the-reverberating-effects-of-explosive-weapons/.

NSU. 2008. 'The "prior use" argument: Establishing benchmarks and implications of historic water use, 1920–1948.' Unpublished. Ramallah, West Bank: Negotiation Support Unit, Negotiation Affairs Department, Palestine Liberation Organisation.

'Number of people who drowned by falling into a swimming-pool correlates with number of films Nicolas Cage appeared in.' 2018. Spurious Correlations. https://www.tylervigen.com/view_correlation?id=359.

Palestinian Water Authority (PWA). 2018. 'Water resources status report.' Gaza: PWA.

Penhaul, Karl, Kianne Sadeq, Kevin Flower, and Mohammed Tawfeeq. 'American among 6 kidnapped in Baghdad.' CNN World (1 November 2004). http://www.cnn.com/2004/WORLD/meast/11/01/iraq.main/index.html.

Pinera, Jean-François. 2011. *Cities, Water and War: Looking at How Water Utilities and Aid Agencies Collaborate in Cities Affected by Armed Conflicts*. Loughborough: LAP LAMBERT Academic Publishing.

Pinera, Jean-Francois, and Robert Reed. 2009. 'A tale of two cities: Restoring water services in Kabul and Monrovia,' *Disasters*, 33: 574–590.

Pinera, Jean-François, and Lisa Rudge. 2005. 'Water and sanitation assistance for Kabul: A lot for the happy few?' Presented at 31st WEDC International Conference. Kampala, Uganda.

Polimen, J. M., K. Mayumi, M. Giampeitro, and B. Alcott. 2008. *The Jevons Paradox and the Myth of Resource Efficiency Improvements*. New York: Earthscan.

Pollack, G. H., X. Figueroa, and Q. Zhao. 2009. 'Molecules, water, and radiant energy: New clues for the origin of life,' *International Journal of Molecular Science*, 10: 1419–1429.

Price, Star, Keith Cornell, and Ted Saad (dir.). *Bullshit! Penn & Teller: Feng Shui/Bottled Water*. March 7, 2003.

Pruitt, Sarah. 'Why the Tennessee Valley Authority was the New Deal's most ambitious—and controversial—program,' History Channel, May 19, 2021. https://www.history.com/news/tennessee-valley-authority-new-deal-progress-controversy.

Prüss-Ustün, Annette, Jamie Bartram, Thomas Clasen, John M. Colford Jr, Oliver Cumming, Valerie Curtis, Sophie Bonjour, Alan D. Dangour, Jennifer De France, Lorna Fewtrell, Matthew C. Freeman, Bruce Gordon, Paul R. Hunter, Richard B. Johnston, Colin Mathers, Daniel Mäusezahl, Kate Medlicott, Maria Neira, Meredith Stocks, Jennyfer Wolf, and Sandy Cairncross. 2014. 'Burden of disease from inadequate water, sanitation and hygiene in low- and middle-income settings: A retrospective analysis of data from 145 countries,' *Tropical Medicine and International Health*, 19: 894–905.

Ramesh, A., K. Blanchet, J. H. Ensink, and B. Roberts. 2015. 'Evidence on the effectiveness of Water, Sanitation, and Hygiene (WASH) interventions on health outcomes in humanitarian crises: A systematic review,' *Plos One*, 10: e0124688.

REACH.org. 2020. 'Secondary desk review on WASH assessments in Yemen (May 2020).' Geneva: Reach Organization.

Redniss, Lauren. 2016. *Thunder and Lightning: Weather Past, Present, Future*. London: Jonathan Cape.

Reisner, Marc. 1986. *Cadillac Desert: The American West and Its Disappearing Water*. New York: Penguin Books.

Robinson, Isabel, and Ellen Nohle. 2016. 'Proportionality and precautions in attack: The reverberating effects of using explosive weapons in populated areas,' *International Review of the Red Cross*, 98(1): 107–145.

Rockström, Johan, Will Steffen, Kevin Noone, Åsa Persson, F. Stuart Chapin, Eric F. Lambin, Timothy M. Lenton, Marten Scheffer, Carl Folke, Hans Joachim Schellnhuber, Björn Nykvist, Cynthia A. de Wit, Terry Hughes, Sander van der Leeuw, Henning Rodhe, Sverker Sörlin, Peter K. Snyder, Robert Costanza, Uno Svedin, Malin Falkenmark, Louise Karlberg, Robert W. Corell, Victoria J. Fabry, James Hansen, Brian Walker, Diana Liverman, Katherine

Richardson, Paul Crutzen, and Jonathan A. Foley. 2009. 'A safe operating space for humanity,' *Nature*, 461: 472–475.

Roy, Arundhati. 2007. *The Cost of Living*. New York: Random House.

Sabin, Paul. 2013. *The Bet: Paul Ehrlich, Julian Simon, and Our Gamble over Earth's Future*. New Haven: Yale University Press.

Said, Edward. 1993. 'The Morning After.' *London Review of Books*: 3–5.

Said, Edward. 1994. *Culture and Imperialism*. New York: Vintage Books.

Said, Edward. 2003. 'The Blind Arrogance of the Imperial Gaze,' *The Irish Times*. Dublin. https://www.irishtimes.com/opinion/the-blind-arrogance-of-the-imperial-gaze-1.367429.

Salama, Ahmad Saleh Auda. 2017. 'Microbiological quality of soaps and efficacy of antiseptics and disinfectants used in hospitals in Gaza-Palestine.' Master's thesis, Islamic University Palestine. https://search.emarefa.net/detail/BIM-735237.

Salih, Tayeb. 1966. *Season of Migration to the North*. Sandton: Heinemann.

Saunders, Trelawney. 1881. *An Introduction to the Survey of Western Palestine: Its Waterways, Plains, & Highlands (According to the Survey conducted by Lieutenants Conder & Kitchener, R.E. for the Palestine Exploration Fund)*. London: Richard Bentley and Son.

Schmidt, Jeremy. 2017. *Water: Abundance, Scarcity, and Security in the Age of Humanity*. New York: New York University Press.

Scudder, T. 2018. *Large Dams: Long-Term Impacts on Riverine Communities and Free Flowing Rivers*. Singapore: Springer Nature.

Selby, Jan. 2013. 'Cooperation, domination and colonisation: The Israeli-Palestinian Joint Water Committee,' *Water Alternatives*, 6: 1–24.

Selby, J., G. Daoust, and C. Hoffman. 2022. *Divided Environments: An International Political Ecology of Climate Change, Water and Security*. Cambridge: Cambridge University Press.

Sen, Amartya. 1990. 'Gender and cooperative conflicts,' in *Persistent Inequalities*, edited by Irene Tinker. New York: Oxford University Press.

Shimo, Alexander. 2018. 'While Nestlé extracts millions of litres from their land, residents have no drinking water,' *The Guardian*, 4 October. https://www.theguardian.com/global/2018/oct/04/ontario-six-nations-nestle-running-water.

Shomar, Reem. 2021. 'Anti-microbial resistant bacteria in health care facilities: Exploring links with WASH—Final Report (Gaza AMR Pilot Study).' *Annals of Global Health* 87(1). doi:10.5334/aogh.3140.

Smith, Adam. 1991. *The Wealth of Nations*. London: Everyman.

Sneddon, C., and B. T. Nguyen. 2001. 'Politics, ecology and water: The Mekong Delta and development of the Lower Mekong Basin,' in *Living with Environmental Change: Social Vulnerability, Adaptation and Resilience in Vietnam*, edited by N. Adger, P. M. Kelly, and H. N. G. Nguyen. London: Routledge, 25–45.

Soskin, S. E. 1920. *Small Holding and Irrigation: The New Form of Settlement in Palestine* (published for the Jewish National Fund). London: George Allen & Unwin Ltd.

'Status of the Watercourses Convention.' International Water Law Project. https://www.internationalwaterlaw.org/documents/intldocs/watercourse_status.html.

Story of Stuff Project and Free Range Studios, dir. 'The Story of Bottled Water.' March 17, 2010. https://www.youtube.com/watch?v=Se12y9hSOM0&ab_channel=TheStoryofStuffProject.

Strube, Thomas, and Kimberley Anh Thomas. 2021. 'Damming Rainy Lake and the ongoing production of hydrocolonialism in the US–Canada boundary waters,' *Water Alternatives*, 14: 135–137.

Swyngedouw, Erik. 1999. 'Modernity and hybridity: Nature, regeneracionismo, and the production of the Spanish waterscape, 1890–1930,' *Annals of the Association of American Geographers*, 89: 443–465.

Talhami, Michael, and Mark Zeitoun. 2021. 'The impact of attacks on urban services II: Reverberating effects of damage to water and wastewater systems on infectious disease,' *International Review of the Red Cross*, 102(915): 1293–1325.

TFDD. 2021. 'Transboundary Freshwater Dispute Database.' Corvallis: Oregon State University Institute for Water and Watersheds. www.transboundarywaters.orst.edu/database/.

Thomas, Kimberley Anh. 2016. 'The river-border complex: An border-integrated approach to transboundary river governance illustrated by the Ganges River and Indo-Bangladeshi border,' *Water International*, 42: 34–53.

Thomas, Kimberley Anh. 2017. 'The Ganges water treaty: 20 years of cooperation, on India's terms,' *Water Policy*, 19: 724–740.

Tignino, Mara, and Öykü Irmakkesen. 2020. 'The Geneva list of principles on the protection of water infrastructure: An assessment and the way forward,' *International Water Law*, 5: 3–104.

Tvedt. 2004. *The River Nile in the Age of the British: Political Ecology & the Quest for Economic Power*. London: I. B. Tauris.

UNEP. 2009. *Environmental Assessment of the Gaza Strip Following the Escalation of Hostilities in December 2008–January 2009*. Nairobi, Kenya: United Nations Environment Programme.

UNESCO. 2019. *The United Nations World Water Development Report 2019: Leaving No One Behind*. Paris: United Nations Educational, Scientific and Cultural Organisation.

UN-ESCWA/BGR. 2013. *Inventory of Shared Water Resources in Western Asia*. Beirut: UN Economic and Social Commission for Western Asia (ESCWA), and the German Federal Institute for Geosciences and Natural Resources (BGR).

UNICEF. 2018. 'Yemen: Attacks on water facilities, civilian infrastructure, breach 'basic laws of war' says UNICEF. UNICEF press release 1 August 2018. https://operationalsupport.un.org/en/yemen-attacks-water-facilities-civilian-infrastructure-breach-basic-laws-of-war-says-unicef.

UNICEF. 2019. 'Water scarcity crisis in Basra.' UNICEF situational report.

UNICEF. 2021. *Water Under Fire Volume 3: Attacks on Water and Sanitation Services in Armed Conflict and the Impacts on Children*. New York: UNICEF.

United Nations Human Rights Council (UNHRC). 2021. 'Human Rights Council holds general debates on the Universal Periodic Review and on the human rights situation in Palestine and Other Occupied Arab Territories.' New York: UN Human Rights Council, 1 October 2021. https://www.ohchr.org/en/press-releases/2022/10/human-rights-council-holds-general-debate-human-rights-situation-palestine.

#United Nations (UN). '12. Convention on the Law of the Non-Navigational Uses of International Watercourses New York, 21 May 1997.' Treaty Series, vol. 299 9Doc. A/51/869.C.N.353.2008.TREATIES-1 of 6 May 2008. https://treaties.un.org/Pages/ViewDetails.aspx?src=IND&mtdsg_no=XXVII-12&chapter=27&clang=_en.

United Nations Relief and Works Agency (UNRWA). 2016. *Epidemiological Bulletin for Gaza Strip*. Gaza City: UNRWA.

UN Security Council, Resolution 2573: Protection of civilians in armed conflict. Letter from the President of the Council on the voting outcome (S/2021/407). http://unscr.com/en/resolutions/2573.

van der Kooij, Saskia, Margreet Zwarteveen, Harm Boesveld, and Marcel Kuper. 2013. 'The efficiency of drip irrigation unpacked,' *Agricultural Water Management*, 123: 103–110.

Waliser, Duane, and Bin Guan. 2017. 'Extreme winds and precipitation during landfall of atmospheric rivers,' *Nature Geoscience*, 10: 179–183.

Walton, Brett. 2011. 'Going the distance, from Ashgabat to Whyalla: 10 cities pumping water from Afar,' Circle of Blue website. https://www.circleofblue.org/2019/world/desalination-has-a-waste-problem/.

Weizman, Eyal. 2011. *The Least of All Possible Evils*. London: Verso.
Weizman, Eyal. 2017. *Forensic Architecture: Violence at the Threshold of Detectability*. Brooklyn, NY: Zone Books.
WHO/UNICEF. 2020. 'Highlights from Progress on household drinking water, sanitation and hygiene 2000–2020: Five years into the SDGs.' WHO/UNICEF Joint Monitoring Programme for Water Supply, Sanitation, and Hygiene. https://www.who.int/publications/i/item/9789240030848.
WICRC 024. 1998. 'Compilation report from Wat-San activities in Iraq.' In BAG/335. Baghdad, 30 August 1998: Evaristo P. Oliveira. Internal communication of the International Committee of the Red Cross.
Wittfogel, Karl. 1963. *Oriental Despotisms: A Comparative Study of Total Power*. New Haven: Yale University Press.
Wolf, Aaron T. 2007. 'Shared waters: Conflict and cooperation,' *Annual Review of Environmental Resources*, 32: 241–269. https://doi.org/10.1146/annurev.energy.32.041006.101434.
Wolf, Aaron T. 2017. *The Spirit of Dialogue: Lessons from Faith Traditions in Transforming Conflict*. Washington, DC: Island Press.
Wolf, Aaron T., Annika Kramer, Alexander Carius, and Geoffrey D. Dabelko. July 2006. 'Navigating peace: Water can be a pathway to peace, not war,' in *Navigating Peace No. 1*. Washington, DC: Woodrow Wilson International Center for Scholars, 65–84.
World Bank. 2009. 'West Bank and Gaza: Assessment of restrictions on Palestinian water sector development sector note April 2009,' in *Middle East and North Africa Region— Sustainable Development. Report No. 47657-GZ*. Washington, DC: The International Bank for Reconstruction and Development. http://siteresources.worldbank.org/INTWESTBANKGAZA/Resources/WaterRestrictionsReport18Apr2009.pdf.
World Health Organisation (WHO). 2015. 'Cholera-Iraq.' Disease Outbreak News, 12 October 2015. https://www.who.int/emergencies/disease-outbreak-news/item/12-october-2015-cholera-en.
World Health Organisation (WHO). 2018. 'Guidelines on sanitation and health.' World Health Organization. https://www.who.int/publications/i/item/9789241514705.
World Health Organisation (WHO). 2020. 'Global progress report on water, sanitation and hygiene in health care facilities: Fundamentals first. World Health Organization, UNICEF Licence: CC BY-NC-SA 3.0 IGO. https://www.who.int/publications/i/item/9789240017542.
Zacune, Joe. 2006. 'Coca-Cola: The alternative report.' Alternative Country Reports. War on Want. https://waronwant.org/resources/coca-cola-alternative-report.
Zeitoun, Mark. 2008. *Power and Water: The Hidden Politics of the Palestinian-Israeli Conflict* London: I. B. Tauris.
Zeitoun, Mark, Chadi Abdallah, Muna Dajani, Saeb Khresat, Heather Elaydi, and Amani Alfarra. 2019. 'The Yarmouk tributary to the Jordan River I: Agreements impeding equitable transboundary water arrangements,' *Water Alternatives*, 12: 1064–1095.
Zeitoun, Mark, and Ghassan Abu Sitta. 2018. 'Gaza now has a toxic "biosphere of war" that no one can escape,' *The Conversation*, 27 April 2018. https://theconversation.com/gaza-now-has-a-toxic-biosphere-of-war-that-no-one-can-escape-95397.
Zeitoun, Mark, J. A. (Tony) Allan, and Yasir Mohieldeen. 2010. 'Virtual water "flows" of the Nile Basin, 1998–2004: A first approximation and implications for water security,' *Global Environmental Change*, 20: 229–242.
Zeitoun, Mark, Karim Eid-Sabbagh, and Jeremy Loveless. 2014. 'The analytical framework of water and armed conflict: A focus on the 2006 Summer War between Israel and Lebanon,' *Disasters*, 38: 22–44.
Zeitoun, Mark, Heather Elaydi, Philippe Dross, Evaristo de Pinha-Oliveira, Michael Talhami, and Javier Cordoba. 2017. 'Urban warfare ecology: A study of water supply in Basrah,' *International Journal of Urban and Regional Research*, 41: 904–925.

Zeitoun, Mark, C. Messerschmid, and S. Attili. 2009. 'Asymmetric abstraction and allocation: The Israeli-Palestinian water pumping record.' *Ground Water,* 47(1): 146–160.

Zeitoun, Mark, Naho Mirumachi, and Jeroen Warner. 2020. *Water Conflicts: Analysis for Transformation.* New York: Oxford University Press.

Zipper, S. C., F. Jaramillo, L. Wang-Erlandsson, S. E. Cornell, T. Gleeson, M. Porkka, T. Hayha, A. S. Crepin, I. Fetzer, D. Gerten, H. Hoff, N. Matthews, C. Ricaurte-Villota, M. Kummu, Y. Wada, and L. Gordon. 2020. 'Integrating the water planetary boundary with water management from local to global scales,' *Earths Future,* 8: e2019EF001377.

Index

For the benefit of digital users, indexed terms that span two pages (e.g., 52–53) may, on occasion, appear on only one of those pages.

Figures and boxes are indicated by *f* and *b* following the paragraph number.

1959 Nile Agreement, 87–89

absolute territorial sovereignty, 93
aflaj system, 22, 37–38
Agricultural (Neolithic) Revolution, 21
Ain al-Fijah spring, 19
Akkadian civilisation, 21
Allan, Tony, 12, 13*f*, 77. *See also* virtual water
al-Sabouni, Marwa, 52
Amazon River, 42
Amiraley, Omar, 83n.18
Amnesty International, 72
Amu Darya River, 25
Ancient Egypt, 86
antibiotics apocalypse, 69
antimicrobial resistance, 69–70
aqueducts, 22–23
aquifers, 3, 11, 11*b*
　in Gaza, 68–69
　saving water mindset, 16–17
Archimedean screws, 38, 38*f*, 86
Asmal, Khader, 30
asparagus, 24–25, 41–42, 41*f*
Aswan High Dam, 28*b*, 87
Aswan Low Dam, 28*b*
Atatürk Dam, 18, 83, 84
atmospheric rivers, 16

Baghdad, Iraq, 36
Bain al nahrein, 82–83
Barada River, 19
Basra, Iraq, 64–65, 66–67, 84
Bell, Herman, 86
Berlin Rules, 93–94
big man syndrome, 26n.6
biophysical water scarcity, 17–18
biospheres of war, 53–54, 58, 68–70
blooming deserts. *See* desert bloom syndrome
Blue Nile, 86
bottled water, 47–50
Broad Street Pump, Soho, 3, 23–24, 65
bromate, 43–44
Bronze Age, 21

Cadillac Desert, California (Reisner), 14, 14*f*, 18, 40–41, 43

camel power, 38, 86
causation, 77–78
Central Intelligence Agency (CIA), 57
Ceylanpinar Aquifers, 16–17
Cherokee River, 31
chlorine, 65
cholera, 3, 23–24. *See also* disease
　Basra, Iraq, 64–65
　Broad Street Pump, Soho, 3, 23–24, 65
　Yemen, 68
Chomsky, Noam, 59–60
civil engineering, 4, 19
civilisations, 21–23
clean energy, 27–30
climate change, 17, 27–30, 34, 76
clouds, 14*f*
cloud-seeding technology, 57
Cochabamba, Bolivia, 36
Coke, 5, 47, 48
collateral damage, 59, 71
colonisation, 17, 30–33, 92
Colorado River, 14, 44
Columbia River, 79
commodification
　political economy, 6
　rain as, 18–19
condensation, 9
Conflict and Environment Observatory, 70–71
conflicts
　everlasting, 52–55
　Quabbin reservoir, 26
Convention on the Prohibition of Military or Any Other Hostile Use of Environmental Techniques, 57
cooperation, 77–78, 79–80, 92
cooperative conflicts, 80
correlation, 77–78
crops per drop, 37–40, 42, 84
cycle, water, 9–14, 10*f*, 99

Damascus, Syria, 19
dams, 24–25
　destruction during wars, 57
　on Nile River, 28*b*
　overview, 26–30
Dams Implementation Unit (DIU), 28*b*

Dar es Salaam, Tanzania, 36
Darwish, Mahmoud, 51–52, 58
Dead Sea, 16–17
dead water bodies, 16–17
demineralisation, 45–46
Democratic Republic of Congo, 65
desalination technology, 25n.4, 44–46, 90–91
desert bloom syndrome, 32, 40–42, 44–46, 87
Dewachi, Omar, 53
diarrhoea, 65–66
disease, 56–57
    illegal tapping, 36
    spreading, 65–67
    wartime water conflicts, 53, 63–65
displacement, 28*b*, 87
Diyala River, 84
dollars per drop, 34, 37–40, 84
drinking water, 11*b*, *See also* tap water
drip irrigation, 38–39, 40, 90
droughts, 17–18, 75
Dublin Principles, 33–34
Dubrovnik Statement, 93–94
Dust Bowl, 17
dysentery, 65

ecocide, 57, 70–71
eco-determinism, 78n.10
ecoscarcity, 17
Egypt, 21, 85. *See also* Gaza; Nile River
    colonisation of, 30–31, 59
    international water law, 95
    Nile Basin Initiative (NBI), 80, 88–89
el Alto, Bolivia, 36
electric-driven booster, 25
electricity, 26, 27
environmental determinism, 78
Environmental Modification Techniques (ENMOD), 57
epidemiology, 23–24, 65
equitable access, 34–37
Ethiopia, 32
ethnic cleansing, 59–62
Euphrates River, 18, 21, 82–85
evaporation
    human activity affecting, 14*f*
    irrigation water, 16
    overview, 9–11
    shade balls, 43–44

farmers and farming, 90
    aquifers for, 11*b*
    droughts affecting, 17
    in Iraq, 84–85
    in Sudan, 87–88
    virtual water footprint of, 13*f*

Fertile Crescent, 21
Fiji water, 48
financial interests, 33–42
    from crops per drop to dollars per drop, 37–40
    desert bloom syndrome, 40–42
    water for wealthy, 34–37
Flint, Michigan, 37
'Flood in Ba'ath Country' (documentary), 83n.18
food, 13*f*, *See also* farmers and farming
fossil fuels, 35
Framework Agreement, 89
France, Anatole, 93–94
Friedman, Thomas, 78n.8
fruit drinks, 49*f*
furrow irrigation, 38–39

Gabčíkovo–Nagymaros, 94–95
Ganges civilisation, 21
Ganges River, 21, 30–31, 77
gas phase, 9
Gaza, 53, 63*f*, 68–70
Geneva Conventions, 70–71
Geneva Lake, 79
Geneva Water Hub, 70–71
genocide, 17, 31
geographic nationalism, 3–4
Gilgel Gibe dams, 32
global water community, 33–34
global water crisis, 15
Golden Arches Theory of Conflict Prevention, 78n.8
Grand Ethiopian Renaissance Dam (GERD), 26–27, 28*b*, 32, 87–88
Great Depression, 17, 31
Great Influenza pandemic, 56–57
Great Man-Made River, Libya, 25, 63–64
Great March of Return demonstrations, 69
green water, 12
groundwater, 3, 11, 14*f*

Haditha Dam, 83
Harvey, David, 17
Hasankeyf, Turkey, 83
Hays, James, 32
health, 23–24
Helsinki Rules, 93–94
Herero people, 17
hoarding, 75
    on Jordan, 90–93
    on Nile, 85–89
    on Tigris and Euphrates, 82–85
hops, 12
Huleh marshes, 81, 90
humanitarians, 54–55, 58
Human Rights Watch, 72

humans
  water cycle affected by, 14f
  water weight in, 12–13
hydraulic missions, 24f
  of downstream states, 81–82
  hydraulic societies, 21–23
  infrastructure, 25–30
  lubricating colonisation, 30–33
  supply, 23–25
hydraulics, 4
hydraulic societies, 21–23
hydrocycles, 9–14, 39–40
hydro-nationalism, 26n.6
hydropower, 26–30

Ica Valley, Peru, 41–42, 41f
Ilisu Dam, 83, 93
illegal tapping, 36
importation, 24–25, 46–47
incidental damage, 59, 71
India, 26
Indus River, 21, 79
Indus Valley civilisation, 21
infiltration, 14f
infrastructure
  destruction during wars, 58–59
  overview, 25–30
International Court of Justice, 94–95
International Covenant on Economic, Social and Cultural Rights, 35
International Criminal Court, 72
International Humanitarian Law, 70–73
International Law Association, 93–94
International Law Commission, 93–94
international political economy theory, 79
international water conflicts, 74–95
  Colorado River, 44
  hoarding on Jordan, 90–93
  hoarding on Nile, 85–89
  hoarding on Tigris and Euphrates, 82–85
  not leading to war over, 75–77
  peace, reasons for not making, 77–80
  reasons for conflict, 81–82
  rules for sharing water, 93–95
invisible hand, 35, 38f, 84–85
Iraq invasion, 84
Iraq–Turkey memorandum of understanding (MOU), 85
irrigation, 37–40, 38f, 84
Israel, 81. *See also* Jordan River
  desalination technology, 45–46
  drip irrigation, 38–39
  Joint Water Committee (JWC), 61–62, 91–93
  Oslo II Agreement, 59–61, 80, 90–91
  Summer War, 58
  TVA on the Jordan, 32, 45

Jevons Pardox, 40
Joint Water Committee (JWC), 61–62, 91–93
Jordan River, 32
  cost of water, 36
  hoarding on, 90–93
  pilgrimages to, 77

Kamal Khan dam, 81
Karakum Canal, 25
Kuwait, 66

LADWP (Los Angeles Department of Water and Power), 43–44
Lake Chad, 40–41
land, 16
Laws of Armed Conflict, 70–71
The Least of All Possible Evils (Weizman), 71
Lebanon, 58–59
levers, 86
light, 8
limestone caverns, 11b
liquid phase, 9
local water problems, 15–17
Los Angeles, California, 14
Lowdermilk, Walter, 32, 45

Madrid Declaration, 93–94
Manasir people, 28b, 87, 88f
marketing, 48–50
Massafer Yatta, Palestine, 90
McCaffrey, Steve, 94
Mekong River, 32
Meroitic civilisation, 21
Merowe Dam, 28b, 87–88
Mesopotamia, 82–83
meteorological warfare, 57
military lawyers, 73
milk, 49f
mineral water, 45
Mirumachi, Naho, 80
Möhne River, 57
molecules, 8
Molle, François, 40
monsoons, 10–11
Mumbai, India, 36

Namib Desert, 17
Nasser Lake, 87
Nasser's pyramids, 28b
National Water Carrier (Israel), 90
Native Americans, 17, 31
NATO (North Atlantic Treaty Organization), 63–64
natural resources, 15, 24–25
Negev Desert, 45
Neolithic (Agricultural) Revolution, 21

Nestlé, 47, 48
New York Resolution, 93–94
Nile Basin Initiative (NBI), 80, 88–89
Nile River, 21, 77
   colonisation and, 30–31
   dams on, 28b
   hoarding on, 85–89
nongovernmental organisations (NGOs), 4, 15, 27, 84–85
normal water, 34
North Atlantic Treaty Organization (NATO), 63–64
Norway, 27
Nubian civilisation, 21, 28b
Nubian Sandstone Aquifer, 25

Oglala (Ogallala) Lake, 16–17
Oriental Despotism (Wittfogel), 22n.1
Oslo II Agreement, 59–61, 80, 90–91

Palestine Liberation Organisation (PLO), 90
Palestinian Water Authority (PWA), 60–61
Palestinian West Bank, 4, 32, 59–61
peace, 77–80
   confusing correlation with causation, 77–78
   lazy thinking about 'cooperation,' 79–80
peak water, 15
Pepsi, 48
Perrier, 48
Peruvian asparagus, 24–25, 41–42, 41f
petrol-driven booster, 25
pivot irrigation, 38–39
planetary boundaries, 15–16
plant uptake, 12
pograms, 55
political ecology theory, 79, 92
political economy, 6, 14f
pollution, 16–17, 16n.11, 22–23
Poopó Lake, 16–17
population bomb, 15
precipitation, 9, 14f
precipitation-sheds, 16
primordialism, 52
private sector, 33, 34–35, 37
propaganda ministries, 18
public health, 23–24, 65
pumping technology, 24–25, 66, 86

rain
   as commodity, 18–19, 33–34
   right to capture, 4–5
Rainy Lake, 31n.19
recession agriculture, 86
Reisner, Mark, 14
religious rituals, 77

remineralisation, 45–46, 90
Republic of Congo, 11b
reservoirs
   destruction of, 58–59
   names of, 24–25
   shade balls, 43–44
resettlement villages, 28b
Resolution 2573, 70–72
reverse osmosis (RO), 45
ripples, 8, 20
'Ritual of the Calling of an Engineer' (Kipling), 4n.2
rivers, 3, 56
Riverscope method, 27n.13
Rockström, Johan, 15–16
Rogun Dam, 26–27
Roman Empire, 22–23
Roy, Arundhati, 26
Ruhr River, 57
rules, for sharing water, 93–95
Rules of War, 70–73, 92
Rwanda, 65

Sahara Desert, 25
Said, Edward, 59–60
Salih, Tayeb, 86
salinity levels, 84
Salish Sea, 31n.19
Salzburg Resolution, 93–94
San Pellegrino, 48
Sarajevo, Bosnia and Herzegovina, 58
satiating thirst, 20–50
   financial interests, 33–42
   hydraulic missions, 21–33
   solutionism, 42–50
Save the Tigris, 84–85
saving water, 15
scarcity, water, 17–18
sediment, 87
Selby, Jan, 61–62
Sen, Amartya, 80
Seoul Rules, 93–94
sewage, 63f, 64, 65–66, 68–70
shade balls, 43–44
sharing water, 93–95
Shatt al-Arab river, 84
Sinai Desert, 68–69
Smith, Adam, 35, 38f
Snow, John, 23–24, 65
social water scarcity, 17–18, 21
soft drinks industry, 47, 49f
soil water, 12, 14f
solid phase, 9
solutionism, 42–50
   bottled water, 47–50
   desalting sea to bloom desert, 44–46

shade balls, 43–44
sugar water, 46–47
Spanish flu, 65
spring water, 11b
stealing, 36
submersible pumps, 25
Sudan, 28b
sugar water, 46–47
Sumerian civilisation, 21
summer hydrocycle diagram, 10–11
Summer War, 58
supply, 23–25
surface runoff, 14f
surface-to-surface missiles, 58
Sustainable Development Goals, 36
sustainable water use, 17–18

Tabqa Dam, 83
Tana Lake, 86
tanks (armoured fighting vehicles), 57
tap water, 47–49, 62–63, 68–70
Tel al-Zaatar camp, 58
Tennessee River, 31
Tennessee Valley Authority (TVA), 31–33, 84
thirst, 20–50
　financial interests, 33–42
　hydraulic missions, 21–33
　solutionism, 42–50
Three Gorges Dam, 27n.9
Tiberias Lake, 45–46, 81, 90
Tigris River, 21, 82–85
timed systems, 22, 37–38
torture, 71
Toshka Lakes, 87
transpiration
　human activity affecting, 14f
　irrigation water, 16
　overview, 9–11
　shade balls, 43–44
treadle pumps, 38
treatment plants, 3, 19, 68
trench warfare, 56–57, 65
Trump administration, 28b, 89
Tulare Lake, 16–17
Turkey–Iraq memorandum of understanding (MOU), 85
TVA (Tennessee Valley Authority), 31–33, 84
TVA on the Jordan, 32, 45

UN Economic Commission for Europe (UNECE), 94–95

UN General Assembly, 35, 57
UN Sustainable Development Goals, 36
UN Watercourses Convention, 94–95
uranium, 31
Urmia Lake, 16–17, 84
Uruguayan–Paraguayan Pulp Mills, 94–95

vegetation, 12
Victoria Lake, 86
Vietnam War, 57
virtual water, 12, 46, 77, 84–85
Volvic bottled water company, 49–50

war, 51–73
　atrocities committed, 55–58
　cumulative impact, 62–65
　destruction of water reservoirs, 58–59
　ethnic cleansing, 59–62
　everlasting conflict, 52–55
　international water conflicts, 75–77
　rules of, 70–73
　spreading disease, 65–67
　toxic biospheres of, 68–70
wastewater services, 36, 53–54, 90
water, 7–19
　local water problems, 15–17
　rain as commodity, 18–19
　scarcity of, 17–18
　water cycles, 9–14
watersheds, 16
WCD (World Commission on Dams), 30
wealthy population, 34–37
Weizman, Eyal, 71
wells
　Oslo II Agreement, 61
　overlooking in hydrocycle, 11
　used for killing, 55–56
windmills, 38
winter hydrocycle diagram, 10–11
World Bank, 27–30, 80. See also Nile Basin Initiative (NBI)
World Commission on Dams (WCD), 30
World Health Organisation (WHO), 66
World War I, 18, 57, 65
World War II, 57

Yemen, 68
Yser River, 56–57

Zayandeh Rud river, 84
Zombie theory of politics, 78n.10